Listening C1

Six practice tests for the
Cambridge C1 Advanced

CAE

C1

Jane Turner

PROSPERITY EDUCATION
www.prosperityeducation.net

Registered offices: Sherlock Close, Cambridge
CB3 0HP, United Kingdom

© Prosperity Education Ltd. 2022

First published 2022

ISBN: 978-1-913825-61-4

'Cambridge C1 Advanced' and 'CAE' are brands belonging to The Chancellor,
Masters and Scholars of the University of Cambridge and are not
associated with Prosperity Education or its products.

Audio production by FFG Media: www.ffgmedia.co.uk
Actors: Kirsty Gosnay; Rob Holman; Natalie Holman; Sandy Murray;
Tom O'Reilly; Jane Turner; and David and Annie Pickering Pick.

For further information and resources, visit: www.prosperityeducation.net

To infinity and beyond.

Contents

Introduction

Welcome to this edition of sample tests for the Cambridge C1 Advanced Listening, which has been written to replicate the Cambridge exam experience and has undergone rigorous expert and peer review. It comprises six C1 Advanced Listening tests, 180 individual assessments with answer keys and audio transcripts, providing a large bank of high-quality, test-practice material for candidates.

The accompanying audio files to this resource are available to download from the Prosperity Education website (see the end of this book for instructions).

You or your students, if you are a teacher, will hopefully enjoy the wide range of recordings and benefit from the repetitive practice, something that is key to preparing for this part of the C1 Advanced (CAE) examination.

I hope that you will find this resource a useful study aid, and I wish you all the best in preparing for the exam.

Jane Turner
Cambridge, 2022

Jane Turner is an associate lecturer in EAP/EFL at Anglia Ruskin University, Cambridge, and an EFL materials writer for international exam boards, universities and publishers. She previously worked as a Cambridge ESOL examiner for the British Council, and holds an MA in Educational Management and Cambridge CELTA and DELTA.

About the C1 Advanced Listening

The Cambridge English C1 Advanced (CAE) examination is a timed assessment, with approximately 40 minutes assigned to the Listening section, which is worth 20% of the available grade and comprises 30 individual assessments.

The Listening section of the examination tests candidates' abilities to follow a diverse range of spoken English, and to understand the speakers' personal opinions and attitudes, specific information being conveyed and also general meaning of lengthier monologues. It is broken down in to four parts with one mark awarded to each correct answer:

- Part 1 contains three recordings of people speaking in different situations. Each recording is followed by two multiple-choice questions.

- Part 2 is a longer recording of an individual speaking about a specific topic. In each of the eight sentences that follow, a word or short phrase has been removed.

- Part 3 is a longer recording of people speaking about a specific topic. There follows six multiple-choice questions.

- Part 4 contains five short recordings of individuals speaking about a common subject. Each recording is followed by two questions tasks.

In the exam, candidates will hear each recording twice and will be given time to read the questions before the recording is played. In this resource, the recordings play only once.

For more information, visit the Cambridge Assessment English website.

Prosperity Education

Our growing range of tests cover the IELTS Academic and Cambridge English B2 First (previously known as the FCE), C1 Advanced (CAE) and C2 Proficiency (CPE) exam. They are available in print or as pdfs which you can download directly from www.prosperityeducation.net. Each resource has a free sample so that you can evaluate its quality.

    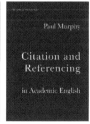

PROSPERITY EDUCATION
www.prosperityeducation.net

Cambridge C1 Advanced Listening

Test 1

You will hear three different extracts. For questions 1–6, select the best answer A, B or C. There are two questions for each extract. Read the questions carefully before playing the audio. In the exam, you will have the opportunity to listen to each recording twice.

Extract One

---

1   You hear two colleagues discussing a staff meeting that has been arranged. What issue do the colleagues disagree about?

    A   Planning time off in advance

    B   Sending work emails after office hours

    C   Asking staff to work at weekends

2   What does the woman suggest about work conditions in her job?

    A   Employees rarely get the time off they request.

    B   There is a supportive work environment.

    C   The company treats employees with children differently.

Extract Two

---

3   You hear two friends discussing the topic of marketing. What is the woman's criticism of online marketing?

    A   It has an impact on consumers' data privacy.

    B   It rarely increases sales for businesses.

    C   It makes using the internet less enjoyable.

4 Why does the man mention store loyalty cards?

    A To support the main point the woman is making

    B To express a reservation about the woman's interpretation

    C To suggest a solution to the issue raised by the woman

Extract Three

5 You hear a woman telling her friend about a job offer she has received. What is she doing during the conversation?

    A Justifying the decision she made about the offer

    B Comparing the advantages and disadvantages of the job

    C Expressing her pride in being offered the position

6 What point does the man make about 'culture shock'?

    A It may affect people in different ways.

    B There might be a delay before people experience it.

    C It can provide people with a new perspective on life.

You will hear a business owner called Amanda Thorpe talking about working with family. For questions 7–14, complete the sentence with a word or short phrase (a maximum of three words). Read the questions carefully before playing the audio. In the exam, you will have the opportunity to listen to each recording twice.

Working in a Family Business

Amanda says her family almost lost their business during the

7)_____ when she was a child.

She thinks the close bond between family members can be an

8)_____ when it comes to business.

She thinks it's essential to set clear **9)**_____ when working with family members.

Amanda gets annoyed when people assume she received

10)_____ when working in the family business.

She decided to take a degree in **11)**_____ after working in her family's business at weekends when she was young.

In her role as an independent consultant, Amanda helped her family improve the

12)_____ in the business.

She feels that working for other companies has enabled her to have a more

13)_____ view of her family's business.

Amanda's branch of the business specialises in **14)**_____, and she believes this is a market with great potential.

You will hear an interview in which two food experts, Mary Palmer and John Hunt, are talking about food broadcasting and publishing. For questions 15–20, select the best answer A, B, C or D. Read the questions carefully before playing the audio. In the exam, you will have the opportunity to listen to each recording twice.

15   What does Mary say about her first experience of being on TV?

   A   It was a let-down after she had dreamt of doing it for so long.

   B   It changed her perceptions of the TV industry.

   C   She was relieved that she was given so much support.

   D   She felt that she had to make up for her lack of experience.

16   When Mary was given her own cookery series to present, she was:

   A   eager to reach a brand-new type of viewer.

   B   confident that the series would be a hit.

   C   surprised that the producers had trusted her.

   D   unprepared for how it would change her life.

17   What is Mary's opinion of current TV cookery shows?

   A   They serve as a reflection of what is happening in society.

   B   Their focus on fancy ingredients puts many viewers off.

   C   Their main aim is to inspire rather than educate.

   D   They are vital in the absence of domestic science lessons.

18 John mentions avocados to make the point that:

    A interest in foreign cuisine has never been greater.

    B the media sets the agenda in terms of food trends.

    C it is hard to predict which ingredients will catch on.

    D People are getting mixed messages about healthy eating.

19 Mary and John have different views about vegan food in terms of:

    A whether its environmental credentials have been exaggerated.

    B whether it is likely to become the dominant type of diet.

    C whether young people have driven its recent popularity.

    D whether health is the main factor driving its popularity.

20 When asked about their future career plans, Mary and John reveal:

    A concerns about the direction their industry is heading.

    B intentions to launch businesses outside their industry.

    C desires to make their industry open to diverse voices.

    D commitments to raising their profile in their industry.

You will hear five short extracts in which people are talking about their attempts to get healthier. Read the questions carefully before playing the audio. In the exam, you will have the opportunity to listen to each recording twice.

Task One

For questions 21–25, select from the list (A–H) the reason each speaker gives for wanting to get healthier.

Task Two

For questions 26–30, select from the list (A–H) what each speaker feels about their new lifestyle.

While you listen, you must complete both tasks.

For questions 21–25, select from the list (A–H) the reason each speaker gives for wanting to get healthier.

A Wanting to take control of their life

B Fulfilling a work requirement

C Training for a sports competition

D Feeling dissatisfied with their level of fitness

E Setting a good example for their children

F Making it easier to enjoy their hobbies

G Preparing for an important expedition

H Wanting to gain more confidence

Speaker 1	21
Speaker 2	22
Speaker 3	23
Speaker 4	24
Speaker 5	25

For questions 26–30, select from the list (A–H) what each speaker feels about their new lifestyle.

A Embarrassed that they didn't make a change sooner

B Relieved that their hard work has paid off

C Grateful for the support of other people

D Surprised at how enjoyable their new life is

E Satisfied they have chosen the right approach

F Motivated by their progress so far

G Conscious of how easy it is to pick up bad habits

H Inspired to pursue fitness professionally

Speaker 1	26
Speaker 2	27
Speaker 3	28
Speaker 4	29
Speaker 5	30

PROSPERITY EDUCATION
www.prosperityeducation.net

Cambridge C1 Advanced Listening

Test 2

You will hear three different extracts. For questions 1–6, select the best answer A, B or C. There are two questions for each extract. Read the questions carefully before playing the audio. In the exam, you will have the opportunity to listen to each recording twice.

Extract One

1 You hear a man telling his friend about his part-time job. Why is the man disappointed with his job?

    A   The boring work environment

    B   The poor rates of pay

    C   The lack of career opportunities

2 How does the woman respond to her friend's main complaint?

    A   She questions the value he brings to his work.

    B   She suggests that he has unrealistic expectations.

    C   She objects to him criticising large firms.

Extract Two

3 You hear a husband and wife talking about a property they're thinking of buying. The woman suggests that the property:

    A   is likely to increase in value.

    B   has sufficient outside space.

    C   requires too much renovation.

4 In the man's opinion, they should focus on:

    A finding properties in a desirable location.

    B improving their current property.

    C identifying their preferred property style.

Extract Three

5 You hear two friends discussing a talk they saw online. What is the man doing during the conversation?

    A Complaining about the lack of information about sustainable fashion

    B Highlighting examples of sustainable fashion

    C Trying to change the girl's mind about sustainable fashion

6 How did the woman feel about the talk?

    A Surprised that there was so much detail

    B Doubtful about the accuracy of the information

    C Curious to find out more about the subject

You will hear a professional athlete called Leo Thompson talking about sports psychology. For questions 7–14, complete the sentence with a word or short phrase (a maximum of three words). Read the questions carefully before playing the audio. In the exam, you will have the opportunity to listen to each recording twice.

Sports Psychology

After being a professional athlete for about eight years, Leo is now thinking about how to **7)**_____ his career.

Leo describes his selection as captain of the national team as being an **8)**_____.

He has grown more interested in the **9)**_____ that can affect performance in sport.

Initially, Leo dismissed sports psychology as just the **10)**_____, but didn't think it would have a lasting impact.

He assumed that sports psychology only focused on self-confidence and **11)**_____ because these help improve athletes' performance.

Leo has found it useful to visualise an image in his mind of **12)**_____, and says this has helped his physical training.

Working with a sports psychologist helped Leo overcome his feelings of **13)**_____ when he was recovering from a sports injury.

He thinks sports psychology helps coaches **14)**_____ athletes, something Leo would like to do in the future.

You will hear a discussion in which two colleagues, Max and Yasemin, are planning a conference for their company. For questions 15–20, select the best answer A, B, C or D. Read the questions carefully before playing the audio. In the exam, you will have the opportunity to listen to each recording twice.

15   How does Yasemin feel about organising the event?

   A   Determined to show what can be achieved

   B   Keen to make it a collaborative process

   C   Concerned that it will interfere with her other duties

   D   Resentful that there has been little guidance

16   What does Max see as the main purpose of this year's event?

   A   Update the staff's professional skills

   B   Build a stronger corporate identity within the company

   C   Identify the best direction for the company to take

   D   Encourage closer cooperation between departments

17   Yasemin suggests that previous events held by the company:

   A   lacked a cohesive structure.

   B   failed to generate enthusiasm in staff.

   C   added to staff's perceptions of favouritism.

   D   repeated the same topics too often.

18 Why does Max mention the example of staff bonuses?

    A To suggest an alternative way to improve staff performance

    B To complain about the way the company treats its staff

    C To argue that staff in the company can be hard to please

    D To highlight a difference between the company and its competitors

19 How does Max respond to Yasemin's suggestion about getting staff feedback?

    A He suggests a more efficient way to do it.

    B He volunteers to lead this part of the project.

    C He doubts it will help them prepare for the conference.

    D He argues in favour of doing it after the conference.

20 Max and Yasemin disagree about which practical detail?

    A The venue

    B The guest speakers

    C The budget

    D The dates

You will hear five short extracts in which people are talking about their courses and future career plans. Read the questions carefully before playing the audio. In the exam, you will have the opportunity to listen to each recording twice.

Task One

For questions 21–25, select from the list (A–H) what each speaker feels about their course.

Task Two

For questions 26–30, select from the list (A–H) what each speaker plans to do after completing their course.

While you listen, you must complete both tasks.

Task One

For questions 21–25, select from the list (A–H) what each speaker feels about their course.

A   The course focuses too much theory.

B   The workload is unreasonable.

C   The course offers value for money.

D   The teaching approach is unusual.

E   The focus on self-study is beneficial.

F   The course content is stimulating.

G   The course offers little challenge.

H   The course lacks variety.

Speaker 1 [21]

Speaker 2 [22]

Speaker 3 [23]

Speaker 4 [24]

Speaker 5 [25]

Task Two

For questions 26–30, select from the list (A–H) what each speaker plans to do after completing their course.

A   Work in the family business

B   Join a graduate trainee programme

C   Set up their own business

D   Start postgraduate study

E   Find a job with an international company

F   Continue their studies in the same field

G   Work in the charity sector

H   Return to their former position

Speaker 1 [26]

Speaker 2 [27]

Speaker 3 [28]

Speaker 4 [29]

Speaker 5 [30]

Cambridge C1 Advanced Listening

Test 3

You will hear three different extracts. For questions 1–6, select the best answer A, B or C. There are two questions for each extract. Read the questions carefully before playing the audio. In the exam, you will have the opportunity to listen to each recording twice.

Extract One

1   You hear a shop manager talking to her colleague about growing the business. What course of action does the woman recommend?

   A   Running a price promotion

   B   Introducing new product ranges

   C   Focusing on customer service

2   How does the man respond to the manager's suggestion?

   A   He highlights its practical drawbacks.

   B   He proposes an alternative idea.

   C   He accepts it is as a simple solution.

Extract Two

3   You hear two college students discussing a lecture. What is the young man doing?

   A   Complaining that the lecture was confusing

   B   Checking that he has understood the lecture

   C   Applying the lecture content to a real situation

4   The young woman expresses the view that codes of practice can:

    A   interfere with companies' main goals.

    B   make companies act more responsibly.

    C   change the public's perception of a company.

Extract Three

5   You hear a man telling his friend about a film he's just watched. What is the man's main criticism of the film?

    A   The ending was disappointing.

    B   The cast was unconvincing.

    C   The plot was confusing.

6   What does the woman think about film adaptations of books?

    A   People must watch them with an open mind.

    B   They can actually improve the original work.

    C   Schools should use them to create interest in literature.

You will hear a local government official called Mark Burton talking about traffic congestion in the local area. For questions 7–14, complete the sentence with a word or short phrase (a maximum of three words). Read the questions carefully before playing the audio. In the exam, you will have the opportunity to listen to each recording twice.

Tackling Traffic Congestion

Mark disagrees with the view that vehicle restrictions in the city centre will

7)_____.

Mark sees **8)**_____ as the most serious concern when it comes to increased traffic in residential areas.

Mark's research has focused mainly on European cities that are similar in terms of their **9)**_____.

He says that placing restrictions on private vehicles is just a

10)_____ to the problem of traffic congestion.

He mentions raising parking charges as an example of a

11)_____ approach.

He says the council plans to invest in **12)**_____ for the whole city within five years.

Mark wants the city to **13)**_____ through measures such as rental schemes and classes.

He says the council will be introducing **14)**_____ in residential areas of the city.

You will hear a radio discussion in which a careers expert called Maria Eccles and a university graduate called Joe Simpson are talking about recruitment. For questions 15–20, select the best answer A, B, C, or D. Read the questions carefully before playing the audio. In the exam, you will have the opportunity to listen to each recording twice.

15   What did the support Joe received at university help him do?

   A   Make his job applications stand out from the crowd

   B   Compare the typical career paths in different fields

   C   Find ways to control his nerves in interviews

   D   Identify the most suitable careers for him to pursue

16   Why does Maria mention maps?

   A   To suggest a point Joe has misunderstood

   B   To illustrate Joe's point more clearly

   C   To provide a counterargument to Joe's point

   D   To show the implication of the point Joe has raised

17   Maria says she has changed her mind about whether:

   A   digital reputation management can be beneficial for jobseekers.

   B   companies should look at applicants' social media presence.

   C   the internet has made the recruitment process more efficient.

   D   video conferencing is a suitable replacement for in-person interviews

18   What does Joe say about his first job interview?

   A   It made him question his ability to do the job.

   B   It proved the value of his academic achievements.

   C   It highlighted his lack of understanding of interviews.

   D   It revealed a hidden talent for communicating.

19   What mistake does Maria suggest Joe might have been making?

   A   Not speaking

   B   Not practising his interview techniques

   C   Not researching the potential employer

   D   Not showing his real personality

20   What is Maria's opinion about companies setting unusual interview tasks?

   A   These tasks reveal a lot about the culture of a company.

   B   These tasks have little relevance to most work situations.

   C   These tasks encourage candidates to be creative.

   D   These tasks increase candidates' anxiety too much.

You will hear five short extracts in which people are talking about their homes. Read the questions carefully before playing the audio. In the exam, you will have the opportunity to listen to each recording twice.

Task One

For questions 21–25, select from the list (A–H) the reason each speaker gives for choosing their current home.

Task Two

For questions 26–30, select from the list (A–H) what each speaker feels about where they live.

While you listen, you must complete both tasks.

Task One

For questions 21–25, select from the list (A–H) the reason each speaker gives for choosing their current home.

A   It is a property with great development potential.

B   Living in a friendly neighbourhood appealed.

C   It was bought as financial investment.

D   It didn't require much work.

E   It has plenty of space.

F   The beauty of the property was irresistible.

G   It is in a convenient location for commuting.

H   It was in the most affordable part of the city.

Speaker 1	21
Speaker 2	22
Speaker 3	23
Speaker 4	24
Speaker 5	25

Task Two

For questions 26–30, select from the list (A–H) what each speaker feels about where they live.

A   Its initial appeal has worn off.

B   It feels like home.

C   Purchasing it was a mistake.

D   The property lacks character.

E   Most people aren't keen on the property.

F   It is becoming too expensive to maintain.

G   The location has become less desirable.

H   It needs updating.

Speaker 1	26
Speaker 2	27
Speaker 3	28
Speaker 4	29
Speaker 5	30

33

Cambridge C1 Advanced Listening

Test 4

You will hear three different extracts. For questions 1–6, select the best answer A, B or C. There are two questions for each extract. Read the questions carefully before playing the audio. In the exam, you will have the opportunity to listen to each recording twice.

Extract One

1   You hear a man telling his friend about his hobby. The woman is concerned that the man:

    A   is wasting his money.

    B   takes too many risks.

    C   has unrealistic targets.

2   The man says his hobby has developed his ability to:

    A   plan ahead.

    B   trust himself.

    C   stay alert.

Extract Two

3   You hear a conversation between a hotel manager and a woman who is holding an event at the hotel. What is the woman doing during the conversation?

    A   Expressing her dissatisfaction with a service

    B   Explaining why she wishes to change her plans

    C   Making an inquiry about an item on her bill

4   The man offers the woman a discount on the:

    A   venue.

    B   entertainment.

    C   catering.

Extract Three

---

5   You hear a sports journalist interviewing the captain of a football team after a match. What point does the woman make about the game?

    A   The coach selected the wrong tactics.

    B   The players lacked discipline during the match.

    C   The opposing team played with more energy.

6   The man says he was disappointed about:

    A   some of the referee's decisions.

    B   his performance during the match.

    C   the atmosphere in the stadium.

You will hear a woman called Eva Milton talking about journalism. For questions 7–14, complete the sentence with a word or short phrase (a maximum of three words). Read the questions carefully before playing the audio. In the exam, you will have the opportunity to listen to each recording twice.

Journalism

Eva says **7)**_____ is the area of journalism most people associate her with.

Despite her initial professional ambitions, Eva now works in the field of **8)**_____ journalism.

Eva describes the change in readership figures as **9)**_____.

Newspapers use **10)**_____ on their websites to enable them to cover stories in real time.

Eva says news coverage is viewed as an **11)**_____ by most audiences nowadays.

She believes that journalists have to show a lot of **12)**_____, particularly when they are at the start of their career.

She says she isn't concerned about the **13)**_____ she receives in her work.

Eva expresses her feelings about unethical journalists by saying they **14)**_____ their peers.

You will hear a conversation in which two neighbours, Richard and Carla, are talking about their community. For questions 15–20, select the best answer A, B, C or D. Read the questions carefully before playing the audio. In the exam, you will have the opportunity to listen to each recording twice.

15 Which problem do Richard and Carla agree is getting worse in their neighbourhood?

    A People parking in the wrong places

    B People leaving rubbish in the street

    C People making excessive noise

    D People neglecting their properties

16 How does Carla respond to Richard's point about anti-social behaviour?

    A She challenges him to provide more evidence for his claims.

    B She questions whether the problem is as widespread as he says.

    C She suggests he is focusing on the wrong part of the problem.

    D She objects to the conclusions he draws about people.

17 Why does Carla regret making an official complaint about her neighbours?

    A The punishment they received was too harsh.

    B She did so based on inaccurate information.

    C It damaged her relationship with her neighbours.

    D It made little difference to their behaviour.

18   What does Richard say about the place where he grew up?

    A   It had a lot of opportunities for children.

    B   It lacked a true community spirit.

    C   It served a diverse population.

    D   It suffered from an unfair reputation.

19   How does Richard feel about local community schemes?

    A   Convinced they could achieve more

    B   Confused about their main purpose

    C   Frustrated that they get little recognition

    D   Pessimistic about their survival

20   When discussing improving their neighbourhood, Carla and Richard show:

    A   a reluctance to offer any suggestions.

    B   a belief in the power of groups.

    C   a negative view of human nature.

    D   an ambition to get involved in politics.

You will hear five short extracts in which people are talking about their attitudes to money. Read the questions carefully before playing the audio. In the exam, you will have the opportunity to listen to each recording twice.

Task One

For questions 21–25, select from the list (A–H) the explanation each speaker gives for their attitude to money.

Task Two

For questions 26–30, select from the list (A–H) what each speaker would like to change about their spending habits.

While you listen, you must complete both tasks.

Task One

For questions 21–25, select from the list (A–H) the explanation each speaker gives for their attitude to money.

A Preferring to save rather than spend

B Enjoying the search for a good deal

C Prioritising the necessities in life

D Wanting to enjoy life in the present

E Seeing how money can change people

F Not wanting to get into debt

G Valuing experiences over objects

H Being taught not to waste money

Speaker 1	21
Speaker 2	22
Speaker 3	23
Speaker 4	24
Speaker 5	25

Task Two

For questions 26–30, select from the list (A–H) what each speaker would like to change about their spending habits.

A Investing in better quality items

B Not worrying so much about money

C Being better at spotting poor value for money

D Going shopping less frequently

E Knowing more about financial markets

F Discussing financial issues with family members

G Being better at managing one's finances

H Reducing online purchases

Speaker 1	26
Speaker 2	27
Speaker 3	28
Speaker 4	29
Speaker 5	30

Cambridge C1 Advanced Listening

Test 5

You will hear three different extracts. For questions 1–6, select the best answer A, B or C. There are two questions for each extract. Read the questions carefully before playing the audio. In the exam, you will have the opportunity to listen to each recording twice.

Extract One

1   You hear a husband and wife making holiday plans. What is the woman trying to do during the conversation?

   A   Focus on practical arrangements

   B   Generate enthusiasm for the holiday

   C   Reminisce about previous travels

2   What does the man say about the cycling tour company?

   A   Its main selling point is convenience.

   B   Its prices are beyond the couple's budget.

   C   Its holidays that cater for all fitness levels.

Extract Two

3   You hear a woman talking to her cousin about the topic of wildlife. In the woman's opinion, nature documentaries can help people:

   A   to see the diversity of the planet's ecosystems.

   B   to feel a greater emotional connection with wild animals.

   C   to understand the role they play in environmental destruction.

4 What aspect of wildlife protection do the cousins agree about?

    A Setting stricter controls on the wildlife trade

    B Prioritising the most endangered species

    C Using upsetting images to raise public awareness

Extract Three

5 You hear a man telling his friend about starting university. What is his main complaint about university life?

    A The university doesn't offer enough social activities.

    B He doesn't like living in shared accommodation.

    C He doesn't have much in common with his classmates.

6 How does the woman respond to her friend's complaint?

    A She resents him making assumptions about other people.

    B She suspects he hasn't explored enough options.

    C She worries he will miss out on key university experiences.

You will hear a student called Steven Watson talking about a local tree-planting scheme he studied as part of his university course. For questions 7–14, complete the sentence with a word or short phrase (a maximum of three words). Read the questions carefully before playing the audio. In the exam, you will have the opportunity to listen to each recording twice.

City Tree-planting Scheme

Steven first discovered the scheme during a course he took on

7)_____ in the second year of his degree.

The course presented the tree-planting scheme as an example of

8)_____, to be compared with other approaches to

conservation.

Steven initially thought the scheme's focus on **9)**_____ was

unlikely to have much impact.

Local businesses provided **10)**_____ for the scheme, while the

conservation group were in charge of other aspects of the project.

The use of cherry and apple trees in the scheme reflected the desire to

11)_____ in the city.

Steven uses the word **12)**_____ to describe how he felt about

what the scheme managed to achieve.

For practical reasons, he decided to use **13)**_____ to carry out

the second part of his research.

Steven was particularly impressed by the **14)**_____ benefits of

the scheme, an aspect he hadn't considered previously.

You will hear an interview in which two education experts called John Preston and Sue Jones are talking about their work. For questions 15–20, select the best answer A, B, C or D. Read the questions carefully before playing the audio. In the exam, you will have the opportunity to listen to each recording twice.

15   What does John suggest about the first e-learning course he took?

    A   The instructor adapted their teaching methods for the context.

    B   The subject was unsuitable for an online course.

    C   The success of the course depended on student participation.

    D   The students knew what to expect from the course.

16   John thinks the main challenge for students switching to online courses is:

    A   using the technology effectively.

    B   keeping up with a faster pace of learning.

    C   having sufficient discipline to complete the tasks.

    D   getting used to a more self-directed learning role.

17   John uses the example of online surveys to make the point that:

    A   it is important for instructors to understand their learners' needs.

    B   synchronous courses may be more interactive than asynchronous courses.

    C   instructors can use a variety of tools to engage online learners.

    D   the best online courses combine synchronous and asynchronous elements.

18   When she was offered her first management role, Sue felt:

    A   determined to gain the trust of external stakeholders.

    B   reluctant to introduce major organisational changes.

    C   guilty about having to reduce her teaching duties.

    D   nervous about the demands of her new position.

19   How does Sue respond to the question about the teaching award?

    A   She emphasises that it celebrates innovative methods.

    B   She admits that it favours schools with better resources.

    C   She questions its influence on students' performance.

    D   She explains its value for teacher recruitment.

20   When discussing education, John and Sue have different views about:

    A   what frustrates them about their current roles.

    B   what they see as educational priorities.

    C   what inspired them to become teachers.

    D   what they intend to do in the future.

You will hear five short extracts in which people are talking about making important decisions. Read the questions carefully before playing the audio. In the exam, you will have the opportunity to listen to each recording twice.

Task One

For questions 21–25, select from the list (A–H) the reason each speaker gives for their decision.

Task Two

For questions 26–30, select from the list (A–H) what each speaker feels about their decision.

While you listen, you must complete both tasks.

Task One

For questions 21–25, select from the list (A–H) the reason each speaker gives for their decision.

A Wanting a new challenge

B Guidance from family

C Not wanting to ruin a friendship

D Having no other alternatives

E Wanting to make a difference

F Financial reasons

G Choosing the easy option

H Needing a more relaxing life

Speaker 1 | 21

Speaker 2 | 22

Speaker 3 | 23

Speaker 4 | 24

Speaker 5 | 25

Task Two

For questions 26–30, select from the list (A–H) what each speaker feels about their decision.

A Motivated to set more ambitious goals

B Worried they made the wrong decision

C Hopeful about future career prospects

D Grateful for the improved work-life balance

E Relieved the process went smoothly

F Surprised at how little it has changed things

G Confident things will eventually improve

H Amazed at what they have achieved

Speaker 1 | 26

Speaker 2 | 27

Speaker 3 | 28

Speaker 4 | 29

Speaker 5 | 30

Cambridge
C1 Advanced
Listening

Test 6

Part 1

You will hear three different extracts. For questions 1–6, select the best answer A, B or C. There are two questions for each extract. Read the questions carefully before playing the audio. In the exam, you will have the opportunity to listen to each recording twice.

| Extract One |

1   You hear two friends talking about life coaching. In the woman's opinion, life coaching has the greatest impact on:

  A   getting people to change their long-term habits.

  B   identifying the root cause of people's problems.

  C   encouraging people to set more realistic goals.

2   Why does the woman mention housework?

  A   To extend her point to a different context

  B   To show an exception to her argument

  C   To make her point easier to understand

| Extract Two |

3   You hear two friends talking about improving their language skills. Which issue do they have similar opinions about?

  A   Which types of vocabulary they need to learn

  B   How much work they want to do outside class

  C   Whether someone correcting their mistakes is helpful

4 What has surprised the man about his lessons with a private tutor?

    A They cover an enjoyable range of topics.

    B They reveal many gaps in his knowledge.

    C They motivate him to do additional practice.

Extract Three

5 You hear two friends talking about gifts. What does the woman think about giving people cash as a gift?

    A She wishes it were more socially acceptable.

    B She fears it causes misunderstandings.

    C She believes it shows a lack of thought.

6 The man and woman agree that they should get their friend something:

    A she should keep for special occasions.

    B she can put to practical use.

    C she will remember as an experience.

You will hear a doctor called Penelope Madden talking about ancient remedies. For questions 7–14, complete the sentence with a word or short phrase (a maximum of three words). Read the questions carefully before playing the audio. In the exam, you will have the opportunity to listen to each recording twice.

Ancient Medicine

Dr Madden uses the word **7)**_____ to describe the approach to medical research she supports.

She argues against the idea that historical medical treatments had no

8)_____.

She finds it interesting that scientists are now **9)**_____ treatments from the past.

When studying ancient medicine, Dr Madden says it's essential to think about the **10)**_____ in order to understand the treatments.

Originally, Dr Madden's team consulted colleagues in other faculties because they needed **11)**_____ help with the source materials.

The team also benefitted from their colleagues' explanations of the

12)_____ of certain ingredients around the world.

Dr Madden says that any **13)**_____ substances found in the ancient treatments would not be prescribed nowadays.

She gives the example of **14)**_____ to show that when ancient treatments are updated, they have a role to play in modern healthcare.

You will hear an interview in which two theatre performers, Karl Myers and Lucy Westbrook, are talking about their work. For questions 15–20, select the best answer A, B, C, or D. Read the questions carefully before playing the audio. In the exam, you will have the opportunity to listen to each recording twice.

15   Karl and Lucy agree that their current theatre production:

    A   has been the most challenging one they have worked on.

    B   is more likely to be a critical than commercial success.

    C   will surprise audiences familiar with their previous work.

    D   deals with a classic subject in an unusual way.

16   What does Lucy say about her previous play?

    A   She wanted a role in which she could show her musical skills.

    B   She instantly understood the character when she read the script.

    C   The role mattered less than working with a director she admired.

    D   The part evolved when she gave her input during the rehearsal.

17   When discussing careers in acting, Lucy expresses frustration that:

    A   certain types of performing arts gain more respect than others.

    B   many performers are discouraged from pursuing their dreams.

    C   there are limited creative opportunities outside major cities.

    D   performers get little advice about planning their long-term careers.

18   What is Karl's view of most performing arts degrees?

    A   They improve people's chances of working with leading names.

    B   They fail to prepare people for the practical side of the industry.

    C   They attract people from a diverse range of backgrounds.

    D   They force people to focus on a narrow range of creative styles.

19   How does Karl respond to Lucy's comment about professional athletes?

    A   He objects to her complaining about the difficulties of her job.

    B   He argues that it is only relevant to famous athletes and actors.

    C   He is uncomfortable comparing actors with athletes.

    D   He agrees that people have an unrealistic view of some jobs.

20   What does Karl consider to be his greatest asset as a performer?

    A   Adding something unique to each part he plays

    B   Being able to change his physical appearance easily

    C   Finding a positive quality in every type of role

    D   Having the confidence to play unpleasant characters

Part 4

Test 6
Audio track: C1_Listening_6_4.mp3

You will hear five short extracts in which people are talking about learning to drive. Read the questions carefully before playing the audio. In the exam, you will have the opportunity to listen to each recording twice.

Task One

For questions 21–25, select from the list (A–H) the reason each speaker gives for learning to drive.

Task Two

For questions 26–30, select from the list (A–H) what each speaker feels about driving.

While you listen, you must complete both tasks.

For questions 21–25, select from the list (A–H) the reason each speaker gives for learning to drive.

A Out of personal interest in cars

B To gain more freedom

C Lack of public transport in the local area

D To provide support to the family

E In preparation for an upcoming trip

F To fulfil a lifelong ambition

G To improve their career prospects

H To feel like a responsible adult

Speaker 1   21

Speaker 2   22

Speaker 3   23

Speaker 4   24

Speaker 5   25

For questions 26–30, select from the list (A–H) what each speaker feels about driving.

A Keen to be a better driver

B Delighted at the pleasure driving gives them

C Shocked at the expenses driving involves

D Proud that they don't have to rely on others

E Guilty about the environmental impact

F Concerned at how lazy it has made them

G Relieved they can stick to short journeys

H Frustrated at how other motorists behave

Speaker 1   26

Speaker 2   27

Speaker 3   28

Speaker 4   29

Speaker 5   30

63

Cambridge
C1 Advanced
Listening

Answers

Part 1

1	B	2	C	3	A	4	B
5	A	6	C				

Part 2

7	recession
8	asset / important asset
9	boundaries
10	special treatment
11	tourism management
12	IT systems
13	objective
14	adventure tourism

Part 3

15	D	16	A	17	A
18	C	19	B	20	C

Part 4

21	G	22	B	23	E
24	A	25	D	26	F
27	C	28	B	29	H
30	E				

Part 1							
1	C	2	B	3	A	4	A
5	B	6	C				

Part 2	
7	prolong
8	honour / incredible honour / honor / incredible honor
9	mental aspects
10	latest trend
11	relaxation
12	perfection
13	frustration
14	motivate

Part 3					
15	B	16	D	17	A
18	C	19	A	20	B

Part 4					
21	H	22	B	23	F
24	E	25	C	26	D
27	A	28	C	29	G
30	B				

Part 1

1	A	2	C	3	B	4	B
5	C	6	A				

Part 2

7	harm trade
8	road safety / safety
9	size
10	partial solution
11	stick
12	electric buses
13	promote cycling
14	slower speed limits

Part 3

15	B	16	B	17	A
18	C	19	D	20	A

Part 4

21	C	22	G	23	E
24	B	25	A	26	D
27	H	28	C	29	F
30	B				

Part 1							
1	B	**2**	A	**3**	B	**4**	B
5	A	**6**	C				

Part 2	
7	current affairs
8	print
9	inevitable
10	live blogs / blogs
11	entertainment product
12	determination
13	criticism
14	betray

Part 3					
15	B	**16**	D	**17**	C
18	C	**19**	A	**20**	B

Part 4					
21	D	**22**	G	**23**	B
24	F	**25**	A	**26**	C
27	E	**28**	G	**29**	A
30	B				

Test 5

Part 1

1	B	2	A	3	C	4	A
5	B	6	C				

Part 2

7	environmental policy
8	community action
9	residential gardens / gardens
10	funding
11	increase bee populations
12	staggering
13	electronic surveys / surveys
14	emotional

Part 3

15	C	16	D	17	B
18	D	19	A	20	B

Part 4

21	F	22	A	23	D
24	G	25	B	26	C
27	H	28	E	29	A
30	D				

Part 1

1	A	2	C	3	C	4	B
5	A	6	B				

Part 2

7	innovative
8	merit / scientific merit
9	reconsidering
10	historical context
11	linguistic
12	trade
13	poisonous
14	copper

Part 3

15	A	16	C	17	A
18	B	19	D	20	D

Part 4

21	B	22	G	23	D
24	F	25	A	26	C
27	H	28	G	29	D
30	B				

Cambridge
C1 Advanced
Listening

Transcripts

Cambridge C1 Advanced Listening

Test 1

Part 1. You will hear three different extracts. For questions 1 to 6, you must choose the best answer: A, B or C. There are two questions for each extract.

Extract 1   **You hear two colleagues discussing a staff meeting that has been arranged. Now look at questions 1 and 2.**

Speaker 1   Any ideas what the meeting's about?

Speaker 2   I'm not sure, but there have been complaints about us having to come into the office at weekends.

Speaker 2   Rightly so! It's totally unacceptable to demand that.

Speaker 1   Definitely. I wonder what else is on the agenda?

Speaker 2   Well, I hope someone raises the issue of managers emailing in the evenings.

Speaker 2   I don't have a problem with that, actually. Provided managers don't demand an instant response, it's OK.

Speaker 1   No way! It's so stressful discovering all those emails in the morning.

Speaker 2   I'd rather focus on staff holidays. You know, people suddenly booking time off without any prior warning.

Speaker 1   The fairest thing would be to get everyone to choose which weeks they want to book off at the start of the year.

Speaker 2   Completely agree. But as usual, parents will be given priority because of school schedules.

Speaker 1   Well, I don't mind taking my holiday at another time to accommodate that. There needs to be some give and take.

Speaker 2   But that's my point. It never works the other way round, does it? Who steps up and helps us when we need it?

Speaker 1   Well, we shouldn't blame colleagues for wanting to spend time with their families! We're all entitled to time off. And we should be putting pressure on management to give us the support we need.

Speaker 2   True.

Extract 2   **You hear two friends discussing the topic of marketing. Now look at questions 3 and 4.**

Speaker 1   Look at all these pop-up ads on my social media feed! I just want to catch up on what my friends have been doing, not get recommendations on what shoes to buy!

Speaker 2   Sadly, it's part and parcel of being online, isn't it? You can't really do anything when you're bombarded with advertising. Fortunately, it's pretty easy to ignore.

Speaker 1   But does this type of marketing even work? I mean, I've never been tempted to buy something just because of a random advertisement.

Speaker 2   Oh, you'd be surprised. Apparently, it has a major impact on what we end up buying. But what's more worrying is that companies can track what you're clicking on to get information about you. I think most people would be furious if they realised just how

74

much companies are monitoring what they're doing.

Speaker 1   But lots of people happily give up their private information to companies without even questioning it. Just think about store loyalty cards.

Speaker 2   You mean where you earn rewards every time you buy something at a particular shop?

Speaker 1   Yes. Obviously, you're sharing your data and your shopping habits with that store. If people were so concerned about companies monitoring them, would they sign up?

Speaker 2   I hadn't thought of that, actually!

Extract 3   **You hear a woman telling her friend about a job offer she has received. Now look at questions 5 and 6.**

Speaker 1   I hear you've been offered the chance to work for a company in Paris. That's amazing, Jen!

Speaker 2   Thanks, Ed. Yes, I can't believe I was offered such an opportunity. But I've made the right choice. I mean, I don't even speak the language!

Speaker 1   You're not going?

Speaker 2   Well, I was definitely tempted but I ended up deciding to turn it down. I haven't told the company yet.

Speaker 1   That's a pity. You'd soon pick up enough French to get by.

Speaker 2   Maybe, but the prospect of being so far from home didn't appeal.

Speaker 1   Well, you managed during your degree.

Speaker 2   That wasn't overseas! Adapting to a new culture is bound to be more stressful.

Speaker 1   Yes, absolutely. But you know, most people find it gets easier over time. That was certainly the case for me when I spent a year in India as a student.

Speaker 2   Maybe, but it's the last thing you need when you're also trying to settle into a brand-new job.

Speaker 1   Well, I'm not saying that culture shock is easy, but it can also bring positives. It helped me look at things in ways that I'd never considered before. It really does encourage you to be more open-minded about life.

Speaker 2   Well, I still think I'm doing the right thing.

Part 2

Audio track: C1_Listening_1_2.mp3

Part 2. You hear a business owner called Amanda Thorpe talking about working with family. For questions 7 to 14, complete the sentences with a word or short phrase.

My family has been in the hospitality sector for generations, starting with my great-grandfather who opened a small seafood restaurant. Since then, the business has expanded to include a hotel, and now my tour company. But it's not always been smooth sailing – there was a recession in my country when I was very young, and I remember the family lost almost everything they had worked so hard for.

Fortunately, we managed to come through the hard times, and that's where I think having a close bond with your family is such an important asset in business. When the business isn't going well, it's easier for everyone to pull together. If you're an employee in a company, it might be tempting to find another job when things aren't going well. But when your colleagues are your relatives, you can't really walk away!

While that can obviously be a positive in terms of going the extra mile for the business, working with the most important people in your life can also present challenges. For instance, it can be difficult to switch off from work when you're involved in a family business. That's why setting clear boundaries is essential – you really do need to differentiate between your professional role and your personal life.

It's also worth saying that my family didn't just hand me everything on a plate. That's one of the most annoying assumptions I hear about people who work in their parents' business. You know, people imagine you get special treatment compared to other employees, but that's not true at all. If anything, I've had to work extra hard to prove myself. I started at the bottom and worked my way up.

In fact, I wasn't put under any pressure to join the family business. But of course I was exposed to lots of opportunities to learn about the hotel and restaurant, so naturally my interest grew. I loved working for my family at weekends, and that helped me understand how the overall business operated. I decided to pursue a degree in tourism management, and that opened my eyes to further possibilities in the sector.

After graduation, I expanded my knowledge of the field by working in various roles for different types of business. I also helped my parents update their IT systems, which really helped them run everything more efficiently. But at that point I was helping them out as an independent consultant, so I didn't have a permanent role. I didn't get fully involved in the business until I was in my 30s.

I think having spent time working for other companies gave me a more objective perspective on my family's business, which has been so useful. It certainly helped me gain an insight into the latest trends in the tourist industry. That's why I wanted to take our business into new areas.

I developed my own tour company as a separate branch of the family business. It obviously complements the hotel side of the business very well, but the tour company – called Thorpe Tours – is my particular area of expertise. Thorpe Tours specialises in 'adventure tourism', offering activities for people who want to be active and do something exciting on holiday. There's great potential for that in our local area because we have mountains and lakes, and the sea is right on our doorstep.

Thorpe Tours is going from strength to strength, and the restaurant and hotel continue to do well. Who knows? Maybe one day my daughter will be putting her own mark on the family business!

Part 3

Audio track: C1_Listening_1_3.mp3

Part 3. You hear an interview in which two food experts, Mary Palmer and John Hunt, are talking about food broadcasting and publishing. For questions 15 to 20, choose the best answer: A, B, C or D.

Interviewer: Today, we're discussing the food industry. My guests are TV chef Mary Palmer and the food writer John Hunt. Mary, how do you feel about being a household name?

Speaker 1: Well, when I trained as a chef, TV presenting never even crossed my mind. But it's a wonderful industry to work in. My first TV appearance was actually as a last-minute replacement for another chef. Talk about being thrown in at the deep end! The producers were rushing about, so I had to figure everything out on my own. I was desperate not to let them down. I really didn't want to look foolish on national TV!

Interviewer: And it wasn't long before you were asked to present your own series.

Speaker 1: Yes, that was unexpected! But I did think carefully about whether I wanted to do it because I was so happy with just being a chef. I didn't really want fame to change things. Not that the programme was guaranteed to be successful, but the producers seemed to have very high hopes for both the show and me. Ultimately, I couldn't turn down the chance to make a series for teenagers. This hadn't been done before. The prospect of inspiring youngsters to get into the kitchen was so exciting.

Interviewer Would you say that TV cookery shows have changed since then?

Speaker 1 Unquestionably. People often say programmes are now about style over substance, that they're entertaining rather than informative. But cookery shows have never been a replacement for school domestic science classes. And nowadays, TV shows mirror people's real experiences more accurately. I mean, the cuisines people really eat, and the ingredients they actually use. As the world has become more globalised, so too has our cooking. And TV producers are now covering all ends of the spectrum, from exotic, showstopping food to everyday meals using basic ingredients.

Interviewer I'll bring in John now. As a food writer, what's your take on current food trends, John?

Speaker 2 Well, I'm unconvinced that writers and TV producers determine what the next big thing will be. I mean, from out of nowhere, demand for avocados has exploded like never before, and media content has had to reflect this. Who would've expected that? And look at health food trends. One minute everyone wants so-called superfoods like blueberries, the next some exotic herbal tea! And Mary's right; international cuisines are so influential now.

Interviewer Talking about healthy trends, nowadays vegan diets are all the rage, aren't they?

Speaker 1 Well, it's interesting you refer to it as a health trend. Plant-based diets can obviously be good for us, but I suspect more people are going meat-free out of concern for nature and worries about climate change. At least, that seems to be the primary motivation for many young vegans. I can see veganism overtaking other diets before long, frankly.

Speaker 2 Yes, veganism is closely linked with young environmentalists, although I'd question whether it's necessarily as good for the planet as we might assume. As for it becoming the leading diet, well, I'm not convinced. But I do love vegan food!

Interviewer And what does the future hold for both of you?

Speaker 1 Well, I don't need to be the centre of attention to share my passion for food. I'd rather focus on other people and listen to their stories. That's why my upcoming project actually shines the spotlight on brilliant chefs, farmers and food producers.

Speaker 2 Well said, Mary! The industry can't survive without fresh talent, especially those from different backgrounds. For that reason, with my new food blog I'm keen to work with writers who are just starting out, and give them guest columns.

Interviewer Mary, John, thanks for joining us today.

Part 4

Audio track: C1_Listening_1_4.mp3

Part 4. You hear five short extracts in which people are talking about their attempts to get healthier. For questions 21 to 30, choose from the list A–H.

Extract 1

Generally speaking, I'd say I've always been fairly healthy and moderately active. But I'm going to Central America soon on a geology research trip. As you can imagine, there aren't any shortcuts to get up and down mountains and volcanoes, so improving my fitness will make things easier. I've enlisted the help of a personal trainer who's been tailoring their sessions around my specific goals. I've been pleasantly surprised by how well it's gone. The sessions are fun, and because I'm already seeing the difference in my fitness levels, it makes me want to try even harder. I'm turning into an avid exercise fan!

Extract 2

It's a cliché but I was inspired to become a detective after watching TV shows. But naively, I didn't think about the physical demands of the role! I foolishly assumed you could join the police without being in peak physical condition. In reality of course, there are strict fitness levels you have to demonstrate. Fortunately, my police training course has put together a training plan and there are plenty of people to encourage me. I don't think I would have passed the fitness test without their help. And now, not only can I start my dream career, but I also feel happier and healthier.

Extract 3

I've been working extremely hard to overhaul my lifestyle. I'd come to the realisation my kids were starting to follow in my footsteps of eating junk food and being lazy, so I could see that the change needed to start with me. I won't lie; it's not been easy to stay on track with my new healthy lifestyle. There have been plenty of times when I've wanted to take the easy option of convenience food in front of the TV instead. But fortunately, the efforts I've made have been worth it. My family can see how much better I feel, and now they're adopting the same habits, thankfully.

Extract 4

It's no exaggeration to say that taking up weightlifting has changed my life. I've become so passionate about it that I'm now training to become a coach to help other women like me. Funnily enough, I didn't have any such ambitions when I first took it up. I just wanted to have a bit of time to focus on myself. You know, when you've got a hectic job and family commitments, it's easy to lose sight of your own needs. But I've learnt that taking time out can actually help you stay on top of things and make your life more manageable.

Extract 5

I'm an advocate of the 'everything in moderation' approach to food and drink, and that's served me well. But I only decided to start exercising when I realised I was getting out of breath doing simple things like walking up stairs. I hated the fact that my lack of fitness was interfering with my daily life. I had no intention of training for a marathon, and I certainly didn't want to join a gym. Instead, I opted just to walk more, and that was a smart decision. Setting myself modest goals has helped me track my progress, and it's been easier than I'd expected.

Part 1

Audio track: C1_Listening_2_1.mp3

Part 1. You will hear three different extracts. For questions 1 to 6, you must choose the best answer: A, B or C. There are two questions for each extract.

Extract 1   **You hear a man telling his friend about his part-time job. Now look at questions 1 and 2.**

Speaker 1   How's the new job going? Do you like working in the car factory?

Speaker 2   Well... I'll bet it's not as much fun as your job in the café, but I doubt either of us are delighted to be spending our weekends working! Still, the money's really going to come in handy soon.

Speaker 1   That's the right attitude. At the end of the day, it's just a temporary position to help you pay for college. It doesn't have to be the most exciting job in the world.

Speaker 2   I suppose. Mind you, they've got me doing admin work even though I'd told them I was starting a degree in mechanical engineering.

Speaker 1   What, you thought they'd give you the top job?

Speaker 2   Well, no, obviously not! But I'd hoped there would be chances to work my way up over time. Looks like I was wrong, sadly.

Speaker 1   It's great that you're keen and ready to learn. But the advert did make it clear that it was just a part-time office job.

Speaker 2   I know, but surely they'd want to try to tap into my potential?

Speaker 1   Well, huge companies like that already have plenty of trainees to work with, I'm afraid. But if you're not happy, come and work with me in the café!

Speaker 2   No thanks!

Extract 2   **You hear a husband and wife talking about a property they're thinking of buying. Now look at questions 3 and 4.**

Speaker 1   You know, having seen the house a second time, I'm even more convinced it's the right one. I know it's not got the garden we'd dreamed of, but the house itself is virtually perfect.

Speaker 2   You've changed your tune! The first time we visited it, you started listing all the work we'd have to do to improve it.

Speaker 1   Well, they're only cosmetic changes – no major work. And once we've updated it, it's bound to be worth far more in the future.

Speaker 2   If it were in a trendier area I'd agree, but not in that part of town. That's why we should be trying to find something in a better area. And anyway, I don't want to live far from the shops and transport link, do you?

Speaker 1   I know you're right, but this house is exactly the type of property we'd said we wanted.

Speaker 2   Well, I don't remember saying that. In fact, I'm not even sure I have a specific type of property in mind.

Speaker 1   Well, I suppose we'll have to keep looking. But we really can't keep living in our flat forever.

Speaker 2   I know. No matter how much we decorate it and make it look nice, it's just too small. But if we look in the right parts of town, we'll find the perfect property, I promise!

Speaker 1   I hope you're right.

Extract 3   **You hear two friends discussing a talk they saw online. Now look at questions 5 and 6.**

Speaker 1   So, did you watch the clip I sent you? Wasn't it incredible?

Speaker 2   Yes, absolutely. I mean, I hadn't realised the scale of the environmental problems caused by the fashion industry. All those facts and figures she mentioned were frightening. It's easy to ignore the issue until you're actually faced with the evidence on the screen.

Speaker 1   Yeah, but it's good that the message is finally getting out. And not just about the problems, but also the solutions like sustainable fashion.

Speaker 2   I wish she'd said more about that, especially the part about organic cotton. I'm definitely going to find out which companies use it in their clothes.

Speaker 1   But another approach is renting outfits. I love that because it challenges the idea that we have to keep buying clothes.

Speaker 2   Yes, that was something I'd never even considered. Another thing to research, I think! I'm not sure there's anywhere in our town that offers that sort of service.

Speaker 1   That's true. And buying second-hand, recycled clothes or swapping clothes are also good options.

Speaker 2   You really know your stuff! You'll have to point me in the right direction for more tips.

Speaker 1   Definitely, I'm glad you found the talk useful.

Part 2

Audio track: C1_Listening_2_2.mp3

Part 2. You hear a professional athlete called Leo Thompson talking about sports psychology. For questions 7 to 14, complete the sentences with a word or short phrase.

Basketball has been an important part of my life ever since I started playing it at school. I've been playing professionally for about eight years now, which means I've probably reached the mid-point of my career. And with that in mind, in the past year or so I've been actively looking for ways to prolong my career. I want to ensure that I accomplish as much as I can in the time I've got left on the basketball court.

I don't mean that to sound negative... quite the opposite! I'm very proud of what I've already achieved. I've won national championships, cups... all sort of things. But it'll take a lot to beat being selected as captain of our national team. That was such an incredible honour. But like all athletes, I'm always thinking about the next goal and how to take my career to the next level.

And only a tiny fraction of my time is actually spent competing. Most of my time is spent doing all the things that help me perform to my maximum. As you'd expect, that involves a lot of team training and working on my physical conditioning. Nutrition is another important element, too. But I'm becoming increasingly interested in the mental aspects of sports performance.

I was first introduced to sports psychology at a training camp before a tournament with my national team. The coach had arranged some individual sessions with a sports psychologist. I'll admit that I initially thought it was just the latest trend in sports coaching. I've seen plenty of those over the years so I just assumed it would be replaced with something else sooner or later. But I was definitely wrong!

I thought sports psychology was simply about self-confidence and relaxation. This is certainly a key aspect of it, and many of the sessions focused on that – they helped us cope with pressure, which in turn made us feel more in control at critical moments like penalty throws. After all, I don't think it's a secret to say that most people perform better when they're feeling less anxious.

I now regularly work with sports psychologists. One of the techniques I've personally benefitted from is something called 'visualisation'. You basically create an image in your mind of perfection. That could be a specific move or aspect of your particular sport. So, in my case, I imagine the perfect shot. But a sprinter might visualise getting the perfect start to the race. By developing this mental image, you're training the neural pathways in your brain. This can enhance your physical training, making it more effective.

But there's more to sports psychology than helping athletes during matches or races. When I was unable to compete due to a shoulder injury, I struggled with immense feelings of frustration, especially as I was missing out on key tournaments. And of course, I started to have doubts as to whether I would lose my place on the team. So, working with a sports psychologist really helped me overcome these feelings.

And sports psychology is also so valuable for coaches because it helps them get the best out of their athletes. For instance, having an understanding of sports psychology helps coaches know how to motivate a team or individuals. This is an area I'd personally like to explore when I get to the end of my playing career.

I'm convinced that, relatively soon, sports psychology won't just be something for elite athletes. I think it's likely to become a common feature of sports coaching at all levels.

Part 3

Audio track: C1_Listening_2_3.mp3

Part 3. You hear a discussion in which two colleagues, Max and Yasemin, are planning a conference for their company. For questions 15 to 20, choose the best answer: A, B, C or D.

Speaker 1	I'm delighted you'll be leading our team to organise the staff conference this year, Yasemin. I can't wait to start!
Speaker 2	Thanks Max! I'm glad you're so enthusiastic because with all my other work commitments, I'll definitely need your support. Actually, I really want it to be a team effort this year. The more input we get during the planning stage, the smoother things will run, hopefully. The good news is that this time we can change the focus of the conference, so that's exciting.
Speaker 1	So I've heard. I've got a couple of ideas if you'd like to hear them.
Speaker 2	Absolutely, let's hear them!
Speaker 1	Well, if the company wants to be more innovative in the future, all the different parts of the organisation need to pull together. The conference could be the starting point for that. Let's put the spotlight on how all the individual departments fit into the company's overall mission. I bet there are opportunities for us to help one another if we have the right training. If we do it well, it'll build a sense of belonging and identity in the company.
Speaker 2	Great! Organising the conference around one specific theme is something I'm extremely keen to do. The company's never done that before, which is why the conference can be a bit... well, confusing. It's a shame because there's always an excellent range of subjects that people look forward to. And I like your idea about training sessions. But we have to make them open and relevant to everyone. I don't

want anyone to assume we're just catering for a certain section of the staff.

Speaker 1   It's a tricky balance to find, isn't it? We'll need to ensure that the sessions are informative but also general enough to meet the needs of a wide audience. It's like when the company introduced salary bonuses based on individual performance.

Speaker 2   What do you mean?

Speaker 1   Don't you remember? Some people complained that they weren't being rewarded fairly and deserved more. Others said the bonuses were ruining team spirit because they were turning colleagues into rivals, or at least that was the perception. It's really hard for the company to keep everyone satisfied.

Speaker 2   Well, I'm not sure I see it that way. But it's definitely important to find out what everyone thinks about the conference generally. I suppose we could set up some meetings to get people's feedback or opinions, unless you can think of something else?

Speaker 1   I know it's an important part of our planning, but that might be quite labour-intensive when we've got so many other tasks to do. I wonder whether electronic surveys might be better? They're definitely quicker, and the staff might feel more comfortable giving more in-depth information that way.

Speaker 2   That's a great idea, Max. Would you be able to put something together?

Speaker 1   Sure, I'd be happy to do that.

Speaker 2   Then there are the practical details to figure out. We'll probably stick with the Duke Hotel because it's always met our needs. And I think we should stick to the first week of July. What do you think?

Speaker 1   I don't have any strong opinions either way. In terms of booking the venue, moving it earlier in the year would presumably be a little bit cheaper, I suppose.

Speaker 2   We haven't finalised the finances yet, but I'll bear that in mind. But if we change the dates, that might affect the availability of our speakers.

Speaker 1   You mean inviting people from outside to give talks? I've got to say, they never get an enthusiastic response.

Speaker 2   I find that hard to believe. I'm inclined to keep them. But let's see what the rest of the team thinks.

Speaker 1   Good idea.

Part 4

Audio track: C1_Listening_2_4.mp3

Part 4. You hear five short extracts in which people are talking about their courses and future career plans. For questions 21 to 30, choose from the list A–H.

Extract 1

I'm doing a degree in hotel management, so I knew the course would be mainly practical. When I applied, I was determined to pursue a career in the hospitality industry, but now I'm not sure. I'd hoped that my course would teach me more about other aspects of the tourism industry, even if the main focus was on hotels. That hasn't been the case and the modules have felt quite repetitive. But still, I've gained a lot of useful skills which I can transfer to whatever I end up doing. And I've decided to take a Master's in business to open up more opportunities.

Extract 2

I'm very fortunate not to have the pressure of trying to find work or deciding what to do next after university. I've been given a role in my dad's logistics firm, but only on the condition that I complete my studies. I'm studying supply chain management, which is directly related to logistics and international trade. It's useful, but the number of assignments we're given is disproportionate. I share a flat with three students on other courses, and I'm the only one that has to submit work every single week. I think they're demanding too much of us, personally.

Extract 3

My parents were worried that choosing a psychology degree might limit my career opportunities if I didn't want to work in that specific field later. They're both passionate about business, but psychology was definitely the right course for me. It's intellectually rewarding, and I'm one of those annoying students that loves asking questions and taking part in discussions! And the module about psychology in business was my favourite course, so maybe I inherited that from my parents! I'm even planning to launch a psychology app when I graduate, so maybe I've also picked up some entrepreneurial skills from them.

Extract 4

For some students, making the transition from school to university can be hard. But I'd already spent several years working before my degree, so it was probably easier for me. I didn't just expect the teacher to supply all the answers! On this course, we explore subjects in depth on our own, which I love. Learning to evaluate the information critically for yourself is such a valuable skill. I'll definitely use it in my future career. My previous employer has offered me a promotion, but I plan to work for a non-profit organisation, hopefully in the field of environmental conservation.

Extract 5

When I was applying for degree courses, I wasn't swayed by how nice a university campus was, or how many student clubs there were. Instead, I focused on selecting a course that would maximise my career prospects. With all the knowledge and skills I've gained, I think it's been well worth it, and a very wise investment. I'm now in a great position to be recruited by a top company and earn a place on one of the schemes they run for new graduates. I'm confident that the quality of my degree will give me a competitive edge.

Part 1. You will hear three different extracts. For questions 1 to 6, you must choose the best answer: A, B or C. There are two questions for each extract.

Extract 1   **You hear a shop manager talking to her colleague about growing the business. Now look at questions 1 and 2.**

Speaker 1   Business is slow again today, isn't it? If it goes on like this, we'll have to make some changes.

Speaker 2   You don't mean changing our product ranges, do you? We've been getting some really excellent reviews and feedback from customers about them.

Speaker 1   That's great, but we still need to be getting more people through the door. I'm confident that once people actually give us a try, they'll see we're streets ahead of our rivals in terms of quality and the service we provide.

Speaker 2   So, is marketing the key?

Speaker 1   Well, I've been wondering if we can make our prices more competitive. Maybe we should start with some kind of 'two for one' deal.

Speaker 2   That might work, at least temporarily. It wouldn't be hard to do, and it might buy us a bit of time to think about other strategies.

Speaker 1   Mmm. I know it's not a long-term fix, but I think it could be what we need to get people through the door. Well, I'll call a staff meeting and let's get started.

Speaker 2   No problem!

Extract 2   **You hear two college students discussing a lecture. Now look at questions 3 and 4.**

Speaker 1   Dr Reed really packs a lot of information into her lectures, doesn't she? I've taken so many notes!

Speaker 2   Me too. But it was a really interesting topic, especially the bit about codes of practice.

Speaker 1   You mean when she gave the example of that Japanese fashion company?

Speaker 2   Yes. And codes of practice are about how companies do their business – you know, how they treat their staff, that kind of thing.

Speaker 1   I've seen them over here too. But am I right in thinking she said codes of practice aren't legally binding?

Speaker 2   Not quite. I think she was saying companies can make their own ethical decisions and there's no legal requirement about that. But companies that profit from investment based on these codes have an obligation to fulfil them.

Speaker 1   But in reality, don't customers just want good value and good service?

Speaker 2   Well, there can be a lot of undesirable publicity when companies have a reputation for treating their staff badly. So these codes can have a positive impact on companies' behaviour. Companies might not put them at the core of their business, but at least it's something.

Speaker 1   You're right. I'll add that to my notes!

Extract 3   **You hear a man telling his friend about a film he's just watched. Now look at questions 5 and 6.**

Speaker 1   So, was the film any good? I've heard mixed reviews about it.

Speaker 2   Well, I think you'd enjoy it. And there were some funny bits…

Speaker 1   That's not exactly a glowing review! Doesn't sound like you were very impressed.

Speaker 2   No, I did like it. But I hadn't read the original book so I couldn't figure out what was going on half the time. That was the only thing that spoilt it a bit for me. It wasn't until the conclusion that it all sort of made sense. And the final scene was very powerful.

Speaker 1   I'm surprised they chose such young actors for the main roles. The characters are meant to be middle-aged.

Speaker 2   Well, I didn't have any issues with that. The performers all did a good job.

Speaker 1   I suppose with film adaptations the source is just the starting point. If you go in with fixed expectations, you'll be disappointed.

Speaker 2   Exactly. And some film adaptations work precisely because they do something new with the story. Maybe if schools showed film adaptations of classic novels, more students would enjoy literature.

Speaker 1   But there's something unique about great literature that you can't get from films. It's better to bring novels to life though class discussions.

Speaker 2   I guess!

Part 2

Audio track: C1_Listening_3_2.mp3

Part 2. You hear a local government official called Mark Burton talking about traffic congestion in the local area. For questions 7 to 14, complete the sentences with a word or short phrase.

Good afternoon. I'm here today to discuss what the council is doing to tackle traffic congestion. Now, I know that many people are in favour of banning traffic from our city centre entirely. This would certainly reduce pollution in the area, which is obviously one clear benefit. However, local businesses are concerned that it has the potential to harm trade. I happen to disagree personally, but I can assure you that the council considers the commercial implications of traffic calming measures very carefully.

And some people have expressed fears that vehicle bans in the city centre would simply move congestion elsewhere, like residential areas. This would bring increased noise and parking issues. And we also need to consider how increased traffic in the suburbs would impact on road safety. Actually, this is my main concern since there are many schools in those neighbourhoods. More vehicles in those areas would be a danger to children walking or cycling to school.

We've been collecting evidence from other cities across Europe, and looking at how they're dealing with traffic congestion. We're particularly interested in cities of a similar size to our own. Of course, these places don't all have the same geographical profile. Some are coastal cities, while others are industrial cities in the middle of a country. Nevertheless, we can still gain useful insights from all of these case studies.

One point that has come out of our research is that restrictions on private vehicles can only be a partial solution. The cities that have had the best outcomes are those that have combined these with investment in more public transport. This has to be the key for our city.

So, if we want fewer cars in our city centres, we need to adopt two main approaches. First, we need to provide better alternatives such as cheap, convenient bus services. I call this a 'carrot' approach. At the same time, a 'stick' approach will make driving less desirable. For instance, higher parking charges will make driving more expensive. The city council is working on a range of measures that will combine both of these approaches.

Firstly, the council will be increasing bus services city-wide by 70% within two years. We hope that this will encourage more people to leave their cars at home. We're also committed to ensuring that the entire network runs on electric buses within five years. And we're currently looking at ways to make bus travel more affordable. We are consulting local associations and will make an announcement soon about discount programmes.

And we can tackle the traffic problem in other ways too. My personal opinion is that we need to do more to promote cycling. I'm proud that the council will double the number of bike lanes over the next two years. We'll also be introducing a new short-term bike rental scheme which you can use from an app on your phone. But most important of all, we're going to provide free cycling safety classes – open to all. Let's make our city the nation's number one place for cycling!

Of course, there will still be many people who need to use vehicles around the city. Our aim isn't to punish motorists that have no other option. But if you can use other alternatives, you should. We also have to ensure that motorists use their cars responsibly. So, there will be stricter fines for vehicles parked illegally. We are also introducing slower speed limits on roads in residential areas. And we're exploring whether one-way zones could reduce traffic congestion further.

If you have any suggestions, we'd love to hear them.

Part 3

Audio track: C1_Listening_3_3.mp3

Part 3. You hear a radio discussion in which a careers expert called Maria Eccles and a university graduate called Joe Simpson are talking about recruitment. For questions 15 to 20, choose the best answer: A, B, C or D.

Interviewer	Today we're discussing recruitment. With me is recent graduate Joe Simpson. So, Joe, did you receive much careers guidance at university?
Speaker 1	Yes, a fair bit. Actually, there's so much support available online too. There are some great websites showing you how to make your CV more attractive to potential employers. I also searched for tips about interviews, because that was something I was anxious about. But university careers advisors are fantastic at talking you through how different careers can develop. I'd already figured out the types of career I was likely to do well in, but they helped me see the long-term opportunities for progression each career would have. That was invaluable.
Interviewer	I'll bring in consultant Maria Eccles now. Isn't it great that students get all this access to careers advice, Maria?
Speaker 2	Absolutely! But it's easy to feel overwhelmed with all the information. So I'm glad Joe mentioned the difference between online resources and careers advice services. Some people assume they're interchangeable, but they aren't. As Joe mentioned, careers advisors act as guides, or maybe even the maps people use on their phones. They can help you zoom out and see the whole picture, or zoom in on specific details.
Speaker 1	Definitely!
Interviewer	Maria, how has technology changed recruitment?
Speaker 2	Well, the internet has made it easy for companies to publicise their job openings, and equally, recruitment websites are streamlining the application process. But I'm still unconvinced that conducting interviews via webcams is as good as doing it face-to-face. And then there's the whole issue of social media. Companies are increasingly judging applicants based on what their social media profiles say about them,

something I'm very uncomfortable with. In fact, I can't believe I'm going to say this, but I've started to see the value of 'reputation management'. These services help people optimise their online presence by hiding the less desirable parts and highlighting the more favourable bits. Is this really the direction we want to go in?

Interviewer Interesting! Joe, how are you finding the recruitment process?

Speaker 1 Eye-opening – put it that way! I didn't necessarily think I'd sail through, but I'm more than capable of doing the positions I'm applying for, and I'm usually a very confident speaker. But getting to grips with interviews is another thing. The first time I had one, I was given a problem to solve. I should've been able to do it easily given my university qualifications, but I couldn't. I suppose the shock of the task affected me. Clearly, there's so much to learn.

Interviewer And perhaps more preparation is needed?

Speaker 1 Well, I put in so much work beforehand. I make sure I know what the company does, and identify how my skills relate to the position I'm applying for. I even rehearse possible questions with friends. And in the interviews, I always use the key phrases you're supposed to give. I just don't seem to be getting anywhere. It's frustrating!

Interviewer Maria, do you have any tips?

Speaker 2 Joe's doing the right things, but there's a fine line between preparing well and coming across as robotic or unnatural. It's still important to be yourself, rather than play the part you think the company wants. That might be something to consider.

Speaker 1 That's a good point!

Interviewer Joe mentioned a problem-solving task. What do you think about those sorts of interview tasks, Maria?

Speaker 2 They're fine, provided the tasks are directly linked to the demands of the role. But I've heard of companies asking candidates to do bizarre things, like do animal impressions. I suppose they want candidates to demonstrate their ability to deal with unexpected situations. That's great if you're someone who thrives under pressure. But to me, these tasks say more about the company's values than anything else.

Interviewer Joe, Maria, thank you.

Part 4

Audio track: C1_Listening_3_4.mp3

Part 4. You hear five short extracts in which people are talking about their homes. For questions 21 to 30, choose from the list A–H.

Extract 1

People are always polite about my home and say things like "oh, this is a nice light room", or "everything matches nicely". What they really mean is that it's so dull! All the walls are painted cream and the carpets are beige because those colours have universal appeal. When I'm ready to sell it, I know those colours won't put potential buyers off. I haven't put my own personal stamp on the property because I only bought it as its value is likely to rise in the future. It's just a stepping stone to help me afford my dream home in the future.

Extract 2

Very few people can afford to live in their dream property. Instead, you have to figure out what your main priority is. For me, it was being near rail links so that I can get to and from work easily. When I found my current place, I couldn't believe I could afford something so close to the station. It's a decent size, too. But of course, there was a compromise, which was the amount of redecoration the place needed. The previous occupants hadn't changed anything in about fifty years, so there's so much to do. But I'm very happy here.

Extract 3

We bought our house shortly after we got married. I'd be lying if I said I instantly loved it. The look of it didn't exactly do anything for me. But it was a great practical choice. It was a property we could grow into as our lives changed. It's got extra bedrooms, a large living area and a beautiful huge garden, which would be perfect for children. We've decorated everything exactly to our taste, and, objectively speaking, I can't see anything wrong with the house. But four years on, I'm still not convinced. I regret not waiting until the perfect property came along.

Extract 4

I've been in my flat for about six years. I don't feel particularly attached to it, but I do love the area, which is the main reason I chose this flat. There's a real community atmosphere and I've felt really welcome here from the start. But sadly, I'm not sure how much longer I'll be able to live in the area. My flat has got a lot of faults, and the repair costs are getting out of control. At the same time, property prices around here are rising so I might have to consider living in a cheaper part of town if I decide to move.

Extract 5

I never used to understand what people meant when they talked about having an emotional bond with a building, but I think I do now. As soon as I walked into my current house, I felt like I was destined to live in it! Not that I bought the place for sentimental reasons. I actually wanted it because although it wasn't in great cosmetic condition, I knew how I could improve it. And because it came with quite a lot of land, there was the possibility of extending it to make it larger. It's going to be amazing once everything's complete.

Part 1

Audio track: C1_Listening_4_1.mp3

Part 1. You will hear three different extracts. For questions 1 to 6, you must choose the best answer: A, B or C. There are two questions for each extract.

Extract 1   **You hear a man telling his friend about his hobby. Now look at questions 1 and 2.**

Speaker 1   …and these photos were taken on the trip I took with my climbing club. Look at the views from the top!

Speaker 2   Wow! You've only been doing it for a few months. I didn't realise you were tackling such advanced climbs already.

Speaker 1   I know, it's awesome! I mean, I wouldn't have attempted it if I didn't think I could do it. And the trip wasn't cheap, so I wanted to make sure I was ready for it.

Speaker 2   Yes, you always manage to pick expensive hobbies! But seriously, I know you love thrills – but not at the expense of safety, I hope.

Speaker 1   Well, you need confidence and courage to do any extreme sport, but I still know my limits. If anything, climbing is teaching me to be more logical and careful.

Speaker 2   Is that because you're constantly aware of dangers?

Speaker 1   Well, that's true of all extreme sports. But with climbing, you're always thinking several moves ahead to figure out the best route and anticipate obstacles. It's a skill that I'm using in other aspects of my life.

Speaker 2   Well, that sounds great. Maybe I should give it a try!

Extract 2   **You hear a conversation between a hotel manager and a woman who is holding an event at the hotel. Now look at questions 3 and 4.**

Speaker 1   Welcome, Mrs Jenkins. You wanted to discuss the arrangements for your daughter's wedding celebration? I hope everything's been to your liking so far?

Speaker 2   Oh yes, you've really exceeded our expectations. But would it be possible to add any more guests at this stage?

Speaker 1   How many additional guests?

Speaker 2   Ten. Before we booked this venue, our Australian relatives didn't think they'd be able to make it. But now they want to come. Could you accommodate them?

Speaker 1   There's more than enough space so we can set up extra tables at no additional charge. But obviously, you'll need to think about food and drink.

Speaker 2   Oh dear, that's going to add to our costs.

Speaker 1   I'm afraid so. You'll see the cost per guest on the bill we've sent you. Ten extra guests will change things quite considerably.

Speaker 2   I see. Well, we might need to re-think things and go for a cheaper menu.

Speaker 1   Of course. That's no probem. Now, the jazz band you've chosen is available. But it says here you only want them for the first part of the evening, is that correct?

Speaker 2   That's right.

Speaker 1   Well, in that case, we'd be happy to lower the fee by £100.

Speaker 2 Wonderful! We'd really appreciate that.

Speaker 1 Excellent, well once you've made your final decisions, let us know and we'll arrange everything.

Extract 3 **You hear a sports journalist interviewing the captain of a football team after a match. Now look at questions 5 and 6.**

Speaker 1 And I can now speak to Jack Higgs, Rovers' captain. Jack, that's Rovers' third defeat in a row. What went wrong tonight?

Speaker 2 Well, Kelly… it's been a tough week because we've played a cup match as well as a league match. But I can't fault the effort of any of our players tonight.

Speaker 1 Indeed. But Rovers are known for speed and attack, yet you were set up in such a defensive formation. Even when the other team had a player sent off, you still didn't push forward much. Surely this was a mistake?

Speaker 2 Sometimes matches just don't go your way. We might have had a penalty in the first half, we probably should have. It was one of those fifty-fifty decisions – sometimes the referee gives a penalty, other times they don't. So that could have changed things. But on a personal note, I was satisfied with my contribution.

Speaker 1 The supporters were very quiet tonight, weren't they?

Speaker 2 Yes, it was a shame not to hear them cheering us on in the stadium. I think it did affect us a little during the match. At this stage of the season, we really need their support.

Speaker 1 Jack, thank you for speaking to us.

Part 2

Audio track: C1_Listening_4_2.mp3

Part 2. You hear a woman called Eva Milton talking about journalism. For questions 7 to 14, complete the sentences with a word or short phrase.

Hi everyone, I'm Eva Milton, a reporter at *The Daily Courier*, one of my country's leading national newspapers. There is an immense amount of variety in my job. I've had the privilege of conducting exclusive interviews with high-profile politicians and celebrities, but these don't come along very often. I'm more associated with current affairs reporting, and to be frank, covering those types of stories brings me the greatest professional satisfaction.

There are several different routes into journalism, all equally valid. I originally wanted to specialise in broadcast journalism, as I felt that offered more scope to branch out into other areas such as presenting. But actually, there's less of a distinction to be made between different types of journalism nowadays. Print journalists like me have opportunities to work in other parts of the media.

Sadly, we can't ignore the fact that newspapers are under enormous commercial pressure. I know the publication I work for has seen its readership decline in the last decade. I suppose this is inevitable given the competition we face, not only from TV but also social media, and it's certainly not reassuring to note that rival newspapers are in the same position.

So how is journalism changing? Well, the introduction of rolling, 24-hour news channels has transformed reporting. It's now common for journalists to cover what we call 'breaking news' items, where they report on stories as they happen. Obviously, this is standard practice for reporters in front of a camera. But newspapers can do something similar using live blogs on their websites so that they can describe what's happening minute by minute. This requires a different set of skills than someone working on a news summary for an article or bulletin.

And I also think this has altered the tone of news coverage in line with audiences' changing expectations. Audiences used to tune in once a day or read a newspaper to catch up on what was happening in the world. The news was an information source. Now, however, there seems to be more emphasis on sensational, dramatic reporting. It would seem that audiences want to consume the news like any other entertainment product. This makes me feel uneasy, but I do accept that journalism has to change with the times.

And there are still some key qualities that continue to be vital for anyone interested in a career in journalism. I suppose it's a cliché to say that you need talent and determination, but these qualities do matter immensely. Obviously, the former is a must because the nature of the work requires a flair for communication. The latter is especially important when you're starting out. After all, there is bound to be rejection and obstacles along the way.

And actually, no matter how well you do your job, you're always going to face criticism, and that's fine. People are entitled to their opinion about my work. But what bothers me more is that my profession is one that's often met with suspicion. The perception that we make up stories or intentionally mislead people is very frustrating.

While I'm not in favour of censorship or strict controls on the media, journalists who use unethical methods to get a story betray our profession. Ultimately, it's reputable journalists who suffer because audiences will no longer trust them because of the dishonest actions of a small minority of their peers. It's an issue we definitely need to think about if we want our profession to survive.

Part 3

Audio track: C1_Listening_4_3.mp3

Part 3. You hear a conversation in which two neighbours, Richard and Carla, are talking about their community. For questions 15 to 20, choose the best answer: A, B, C or D.

Speaker 1   Hi Carla, I hope my guests didn't disturb you when they left last night. I told them to leave quietly, but it was pretty late.

Speaker 2   Hi Richard, no, not at all. But thanks for thinking of me. You're one of the only considerate ones on this street!

Speaker 1   Don't get me started! People just leave their cars wherever they want, including places they're not supposed to park. This neighbourhood's really going downhill. It's now almost a daily occurrence that you have to avoid tripping into someone's old sofa or another unwanted item they were too lazy to dispose of properly.

Speaker 2   Yes, and it's definitely happening more and more. How come they're eager to make their homes look perfect, but think nothing of turning the neighbourhood into a dump? It's infuriating.

Speaker 1   Well, you only have to walk around the city to see it's not just our area. We're not teaching people the value of respecting their neighbourhoods and how to be considerate of other people. It has to start with parents educating their kids. Children need better role models.

Speaker 2   And let's not forget things like vandalism. Do you think crime rates are high around here? I feel like they're going up. But what you say about people not teaching their children the right values is a bit harsh. You don't know people's individual circumstances, Richard.

Speaker 1   Well, it just feels like nobody's doing anything to improve things. You mentioned crime, but what are the police doing exactly? Didn't you ask for their help with your next-door neighbours who were causing all sort of problems?

Speaker 2 Yes. But now I wish I hadn't got the authorities involved. If anything, it's made things worse. The neighbours might have stopped their all-night parties, but now they're *so rude* to me. As far as I know, they didn't get into any real trouble, but they seem to think I lied to the police.

Speaker 1 Well, that just shows the mentality of the people round here.

Speaker 2 It's frustrating. I moved here thinking it would be so nice.

Speaker 1 This area might be a popular one, but there's no sense of community. You know the estate I grew up in. It's not exactly known for affluence, is it? There weren't any nice parks, sports clubs or good schools for kids like there are here. But I tell you what, everyone took care of each other, despite their different backgrounds and beliefs. I loved living in such a multi-cultural place.

Speaker 2 At least there are some local groups trying to change things.

Speaker 1 True, and I think word's finally getting out about their good work. What they've put in place so far is great, but surely they could be more ambitious? Why not tackle wider issues? Like cleaning up the parks, protecting nature – that kind of thing.

Speaker 2 Actually, if we really want to improve the neighbourhood, what about having groups of volunteers? We could do the shopping for elderly neighbours, for instance. I'm sure if enough people worked together, we could really make a difference.

Speaker 1 That's the beauty of teamwork. Individual action can only go so far. There could also be creative activities too. You know, teaching people to cook, sew, make art.

Speaker 2 We need people like you on the local council!

Speaker 1 No way, I'm not really one for politics. It seems to bring out the worst in people.

Speaker 2 Maybe you're right. People are basically good, but as soon as they get a bit of power, well, it seems to change them. But I do feel very inspired now.

Speaker 1 Great – well, let me know if I can help.

Part 4

Audio track: C1_Listening_4_4.mp3

Part 4. You hear five short extracts in which people are talking about their attitudes to money. For questions 21 to 30, choose from the list A–H.

Extract 1

Some people are obsessed with their finances, aren't they? Obviously, we all need money for the necessities in life, but ultimately, I think I've got a fairly healthy attitude to money. I don't see the point of trying to invest all my money for the future. I'd rather use it to make life more fun, whether it's nice clothes, holidays or just a night out with friends. But I will admit that I do tend to make hasty purchases. Maybe if I were less impulsive, I'd be more likely to tell whether something's worth the asking price or a rip-off.

Extract 2

I don't earn as much as some of my friends, but that's never caused any issues between us. I think that's because we share the same outlook on life: it's far more enjoyable to do fun activities than just buy endless things in shops. Some of my best memories are of concerts we've enjoyed together and trips to the beach. But in other regards, of course I'd like to have more money for my future. I have no clue about investments or stock markets, but it's something I think might be worth investigating. I doubt I'll ever be rich, though!

Extract 3

I wouldn't say I have particularly expensive tastes – far from it. I'm always on the lookout for a special offer. I hate paying full price for things. And to be honest, I get more satisfaction from the idea of getting a bargain than I do from the item itself! But I'm not great at budgeting, to be honest. I buy too many things just because they're on sale. That makes it harder for me to control what I'm spending. I'm rarely in debt, but given the decent salary I earn I should be saving far more each month.

Extract 4

Have you heard of the expression 'a 'false economy'? It's when the cheapest option actually ends up costing more in the long run because it has to be replaced more often. Well, that's something I need to keep in mind. I'm starting to realise that it's worth spending more on a better class of product that will last for years. I never really use credit cards unless it's absolutely necessary because the idea of owing money frightens me, frankly. I'd rather wait until I've saved up for it instead of borrowing. I think that approach is something I've inherited from my parents.

Extract 5

When I need something, I'd much rather order it online because it's more convenient. I'm not someone who finds browsing in shops fun. I really can't understand the appeal of it at all. I pride myself on being prudent with my finances. I get satisfaction from putting money aside each month and seeing my bank balance grow, and I hate it when I have to actually spend money. I would like to relax a little more when it comes to my finances, though. I probably spend too much time thinking about it even though I know I've got more than enough to meet my needs.

Part 1

Audio track: C1_Listening_5_1.mp3

Part 1. You will hear three different extracts. For questions 1 to 6, you must choose the best answer: A, B or C. There are two questions for each extract.

Extract 1   **You hear a husband and wife making holiday plans. Now look at questions 1 and 2.**

Speaker 1   I don't know about you, but the holiday can't come soon enough for me.

Speaker 2   Mmm... well, let's not leave the planning to the last minute this year.

Speaker 1   I was hoping for a bit more of excitement than that! Aren't you looking forward to some time off?

Speaker 2   Of course, I am. But you need to renew your passport, and we haven't booked anything yet. Where shall we go?

Speaker 1   Do you fancy doing something active again this year? Do you remember that walking holiday we did in Spain – wasn't that fun? Or we could just relax by the beach, if you prefer. Or do a road trip? There are so many choices!

Speaker 2   Ah, yes, that walking holiday was brilliant! Actually, the same company also does cycling holidays – cycling around southern France, for instance.

Speaker 1   Now you're talking! We're reasonably fit, so I think we could manage that.

Speaker 2   Well even if we couldn't, I'm sure they'd have something easier. But the best thing about them is they take care of all the boring planning.

Speaker 1   Really?

Speaker 2   Yes, accommodation, transferring bags, all that. It'd make planning the trip far easier. It'd be a bit pricier than we normally pay, but it might be worth it.

Speaker 1   OK, great. You see – it'll be fantastic!

Extract 2   **You hear a woman talking to her cousin about the topic of wildlife. Now look at questions 3 and 4.**

Speaker 1   Did you watch that programme last night about animal extinction in the Amazon rainforest? It was so shocking. There was one scene where they showed how many species were at risk.

Speaker 2   Oh, yes, it's a great series. They've done episodes about disappearing species in other ecosystems and regions, like deserts, forests, even the Arctic. The scary thing is that most of the damage is being caused by humans. I think that's what these programmes show so well. They really make you see how our actions are destroying the planet. It's heart-breaking to see how this affects wildlife.

Speaker 1   Mmm. But I suppose all those sad scenes can actually be too much for some people.

Speaker 2   Well, I think it's important for people to learn about these issues. But of course, unless governments take action, nothing really changes.

Speaker 1   There's a list of endangered species that they're trying to protect, so that's a good start.

Speaker 2   But it's hard to determine which animals need the most protection. And anyway, the authorities need to do more about animal exports. A lot of wild animals are taken out

94

of their habitats illegally. Why aren't they doing more to stop that?

Speaker 1   You're right. Tougher penalties are needed.

Extract 3   **You hear a man telling his friend about starting university. Now look at questions 5 and 6.**

Speaker 1   How's your course going? Are you enjoying university life?

Speaker 2   Yes, for the most part. The course is great, and my classmates are nice enough, although there's never enough time to chat with them properly. But I'm thinking of joining some student clubs. There's a decent selection to choose from.

Speaker 1   What about the people you're living with in the student flat?

Speaker 2   I don't really mix much with them, actually. They're quite messy and very noisy. I originally wanted to live alone, but I couldn't afford it. I suppose I'll just have to get used to it, unfortunately.

Speaker 1   Well, like you say, there's always a period of adjustment, and maybe you're a bit difficult to live with too!

Speaker 2   Ha! Well, anyway, it's not a huge issue. I mean, it's not getting in the way of my studies, which is the main thing.

Speaker 1   Sure, but university's about more than that. You'll regret it if you don't make the most of your time while you're there. It'd be a shame if you graduate with only memories of your studies to look back on! That's why I think you should make more effort to hang out with the other students in your flat.

Speaker 2   Maybe you're right.

Part 2

Audio track: C1_Listening_5_2.mp3

Part 2. You hear a student called Steven Watson talking about a local tree-planting scheme he studied as part of his university course. For questions 7 to 14, complete the sentences with a word or short phrase.

Hi everyone, I'm Steven and I'm in the final year of my geography degree. Right now, I'm in the process of completing my final research project, about a city tree-planting scheme. I first came across this initiative last year during my 'environmental policy' course. During that module we analysed the scheme as a case study, and it really captured my imagination. I decided it was the perfect subject matter for me to investigate further for my final project.

To give a bit of background, the course I took in the second year was about examining different approaches to environmental protection. So, we studied community action such as this city tree-planting scheme, and contrasted this approach with measures organised through official channels such as local council initiatives.

So, as you can guess, the scheme itself involved planting trees in city neighbourhoods. However, unlike other schemes I'd seen before, this one focused not on planting more trees in public parks but actually in residential gardens. This immediately struck me as an interesting approach, but I wasn't convinced it would lead to any meaningful environmental impact. For instance, I doubted that many people would be willing to take part because it would involve a lot of time and effort, not to mention financial outlay.

However, I discovered that although the scheme was being run by a conservation group, local businesses were actually sponsoring it, and the funding they provided paid for the trees themselves – 2,000 trees, to be precise. Meanwhile, the conservation group were responsible for promoting the scheme and providing educational support to teach participants about how to plant and care for the trees.

These measures showed that, though the scheme was an ambitious one, the organisers had thought clearly about how to make the project more accessible. Initially, I'd assumed that the primary goal of the scheme was to improve air quality. However, while this was certainly important, I came to understand that this was a secondary aim. The group was actually attempting to increase bee populations in the city, which is why the trees selected for the scheme were fruit trees such as cherry and apple trees.

So, having looked at this tree-planting scheme as a case study, I considered the long-term impacts of the initiative for my final-year research project. I began by collecting statistical data to see whether the group had achieved its aims. The results were staggering – far exceeding my modest predictions. Not only had 95% of the available trees been planted, but the group had recorded an increase of 65% in the target species they'd hoped to attract.

I then wanted to gain deeper insights into what participants in the scheme actually thought about the experience. Had there been more time, I would have liked to conduct individual interviews, but this simply wasn't practical. Instead, I opted to use electronic surveys, and again, the overall response appeared to be extremely favourable.

While I'd anticipated positive feedback about how the scheme was beneficial for ecological reasons, that was just the tip of the iceberg. In fact, many participants felt that the emotional rewards they got from the scheme were just as great. They'd enjoyed planting the trees, learning how to care for them and seeing their efforts pay off. They got a great deal of satisfaction from this, and it also taught them to be patient and nurturing in their daily lives. That was a fascinating finding. It's amazing what issues emerge when you research a subject in detail.

Overall, doing this project has motivated me to look for similar schemes in my local area.

Part 3

Audio track: C1_Listening_5_3.mp3

Part 3. You hear an interview in which two education experts called John Preston and Sue Jones are talking about their work. For questions 15 to 20, choose the best answer: A, B, C or D.

Interviewer	Today, we're discussing education. I'm joined by experts John Preston and Sue Jones. John, you're an e-learning specialist. How did you get into that?
Speaker 1	From taking an online course as a student. Although the course materials were excellent, sadly the instructor hadn't considered how to use them online. Maybe they were only used to classroom teaching. It meant nobody could really interact, which was frustrating because the course content was largely based on student involvement. That's why we had signed up for the course in the first place. That experience sparked my interest in designing effective online courses.
Interviewer	From a learner's perspective, the transition from classroom lessons to online courses can be hard, can't it?
Speaker 1	Without a doubt. For instance, these courses are often delivered at an accelerated pace, so time management is a must. Another challenge is staying on track without a teacher monitoring you all the time. Remember, this style of learning relies on real learner independence. Learners have to develop their own study plans and decide how to navigate their studies. I think adapting to this is by far the main obstacle for learners to overcome – far more than technological issues or anything else.
Interviewer	John, it's probably worth clarifying some key terms, such as the difference between

synchronous and asynchronous e-learning.

Speaker 1   OK, well basically, synchronous lessons are delivered live, using video conferencing. And the participants follow along similar to how they would in a conventional classroom lesson. Asynchronous is where all the course material is available online for students to access and complete whenever they want.

Interviewer   And is one better than the other?

Speaker 1   It really depends on students' needs and priorities! Asynchronous courses are obviously ideal for students with family or work commitments, but may lack the feeling of live, synchronous sessions. In synchronous classes, teachers can use lots of techniques and features such as asking learners to complete live surveys. These tools give learners the chance to share their thoughts with each other in real time.

Interviewer   Now my other guest is Sue Jones, a leading educational policy expert. Welcome, Sue.

Speaker 2   Thanks, but I'm still a teacher at heart, whatever my job title!

Interviewer   Aha, yes. So, Sue, was the transition from full-time teaching to management hard?

Speaker 2   At first, yes. Naturally, I was excited about radically transforming the way the school was being run. But I'd be lying if I said I wasn't anxious about the scale of the job. The school board, pupils' parents and other stakeholders had put their confidence in me, and I didn't want to let them down. And of course, I knew I'd miss spending so much time in the classroom.

Interviewer   And recently, you've joined the judging panel for the National Teaching Award. What's the purpose of this award? I mean, can we really judge and compare schools?

Speaker 2   Not at all! The award isn't based on students' exam results or anything like that. It's about highlighting teachers that are doing engaging work with their students using creative and fresh approaches. That's something to be applauded. It has nothing to do with finding the school with the best facilities or staff from the best teaching academies.

Interviewer   And what about the future of education? A big question!

Speaker 1   Well, I'm sure Sue would agree that everyone involved in teaching has a desire to help people. But we need to respond to the world's technological needs. That's a challenge for schools with fewer resources, and a problem my school's already struggling with. That's what I plan to focus on going forward.

Speaker 2   Yes, that issue's going to take up an increasing amount of my work also. But personally, I want education to move in another direction, with more emphasis on global issues.

Interviewer   Sue, John, that's all we have time for. Thank you.

Part 4

Audio track: C1_Listening_5_4.mp3

Part 4. You hear five short extracts in which people are talking about making important decisions. For questions 21 to 30, choose from the list A–H.

Extract 1

Being offered a management role was a great honour, even if it was only on a temporary basis during the head of department's maternity leave. But I wasn't sure I'd be able to handle the role's demands. And of course, the much bigger workload would mean spending even more time away from my young children. But ultimately, the salary increase would benefit my family, which was ultimately my motivation for accepting the role. And I'm so pleased I did. I've had a lot of positive feedback, and now it's likely that the firm will consider me for other promotions or permanent positions.

Extract 2

The best decision I've ever made was agreeing to work on an overseas project to set up a school in a remote rural village. I'd never done anything like this before, but it was exactly the opportunity I'd been looking for. I wanted to get out of my comfort zone and test my limits. I went as a relatively inexperienced young teacher, and six months later the progress we've made has been remarkable. I've been involved in every part of the project and had the chance to do things I never imagined I could do. I'm so glad I took on this role.

Extract 3

If there'd been any way for me to stay in my hometown, I would've done so. But as a researcher in a very specialist field, I had to move to a larger university on the other side of the country to have access to the resources I needed. I was dreading having to move. I didn't want all the practical and financial hassles that come with moving. But I'm pleased that the move wasn't as difficult as I'd anticipated. Finding accommodation was fairly straightforward, and I settled in quicker than I thought I would. I still miss my hometown, though.

Extract 4

Last year, my friend asked me to be her partner in the business she was setting up. Do I regret saying 'no' and sticking with my job? Not exactly. Starting a business is such a risk, and can be so complicated. I just wanted to keep things simple. That was my rationale for turning down her offer. She understood and I'm delighted that her business has taken off – she deserves it. Being an entrepreneur isn't right for me, but seeing her success has still inspired me. I'm now more open to aiming higher with my career goals, and taking on bigger challenges.

Extract 5

This time last year, I had a very prestigious position in one of the top companies in the city. Now, I'm working in a much smaller role, but I can enjoy plenty of free time. When my company announced it was downsizing, I was offered a role in a regional office. It did feel like a backwards step in my career, but it was in a beautiful area much closer to my parents. They suggested I had nothing to lose by giving it a try, and I'm glad I listened to them. I have less responsibility and I'm much happier now.

Part 1
Audio track: C1_Listening_6_1.mp3

Part 1. You will hear three different extracts. For questions 1 to 6, you must choose the best answer: A, B or C. There are two questions for each extract.

Extract 1   **You hear two friends talking about life coaching. Now look at questions 1 and 2.**

Speaker 1   I've just seen Mel. She was telling me about that qualification she's doing, but most of it went over my head. It's something about life coaching, isn't it?

Speaker 2   That's right. She'll be great at it. You know Mel – how many times has she helped one of us with our problems?

Speaker 1   Is that all life coaching means?

Speaker 2   Well, from what I gather, life coaches show their clients how to adopt new approaches or new routines, and this enables them to make permanent changes. That's where they really add value. So, it's about much more than analysing a specific problem and fixing it.

Speaker 1   You sound like Mel! I'm still lost, though.

Speaker 2   Look, take something you're always complaining about. Like, having to do chores around the house. Imagine that you let them build up because you don't like doing them. Well, after a while, the task becomes virtually unmanageable because the house is completely filthy and there's so much to do.

Speaker 1   OK…

Speaker 2   So, a life coach would help you address this. Not by helping you with the chores this one time, but by helping you change your attitude to doing the chores in the first place. By working on your mindset, that will help you going forward.

Speaker 1   Oh, that makes sense. And I agree with you – Mel would be brilliant at that.

Extract 2   **You hear two friends talking about improving their language skills. Now look at questions 3 and 4.**

Speaker 1   Have you seen the article our French teacher assigned for homework? It's full of expressions I've never seen before. I bet they're not even in common use. I think her expectations of our ability are pretty unrealistic.

Speaker 2   I'd say she's got the balance right. You'd be the first to moan if it were too easy. And anyway, yesterday you were full of praise for the way she was helping you fix your pronunciation.

Speaker 1   That's true. I mean, how are you supposed to improve if nobody points out where you're going wrong?

Speaker 2   Some people would find it demoralising, constantly being corrected, but I see it your way. It's like when I'm studying with my private Japanese tutor.

Speaker 1   So, he's quite strict, then?

Speaker 2   Well, he sets a lot of extra tasks, but I don't mind because it's all really fun. If you're engaged and interested in the topics, it doesn't really feel like work.

Speaker 1   And you're improving?

Speaker 2   Absolutely. And while he's done it in a sensitive way, he's made me realise all the stuff I still don't know. Like I say, that would come as a nasty shock to some people, but I see it as a challenge!

Extract 3 **You hear two friends talking about gifts. Now look at questions 5 and 6.**

Speaker 1 It's Ella's birthday on Thursday! Yet another gift to sort out. The constant pressure to give gifts over here is something I'm really struggling with. How is it thoughtful to give someone something they didn't even want?

Speaker 2 Well, if you hate shopping for gifts so much, why not just give her the money?

Speaker 1 Was that a serious suggestion? Trust me, if I thought I could get away with it, I would. But it's just not the done thing over here, is it? Or have I misunderstood how it works?

Speaker 2 You're probably right. Let's pick something together. She doesn't have very fancy tastes so there's no point getting her anything she'll only wear once a year.

Speaker 1 Back home, we do things like going to a concert. Something that's a nice memory to look back on. What about that instead of buying her something?

Speaker 2 I like the sentiment, but it's too late to organise anything. To be on the safe side, I was thinking along the lines of something hobby-related. Maybe some art supplies?

Speaker 1 Actually, I like your thinking. It's her main interest so she'd get plenty of use out of it.

Part 2

Audio track: C1_Listening_6_2.mp3

Part 2. You hear a doctor called Penelope Madden talking about ancient remedies. For questions 7 to 14, complete the sentences with a word or short phrase.

Hello everyone, I'm Dr Penelope Madden, lecturer in health sciences. Now, as a member of the medical faculty, you'd expect my academic research to be concerned with the latest scientific breakthroughs. And that's usually the case. My colleagues and I have access to cutting-edge equipment and technology, and I think it's fair to say our ethos is one that embraces the innovative to move conventional medicine forward.

But as scientists I think it's important to look to the past as well. Of course, with the benefit of our advanced medical knowledge, the healthcare practices of previous centuries may indeed seem bizarre or lacking in any scientific merit. But even so, the fact that these treatments, experiments and observations were recorded is valuable in itself. These insights eventually formed the foundations of modern medicine, after all.

And interestingly, we're now in a phase where we're no longer automatically rejecting traditional therapies. Instead, there's been a move within the academic community towards reconsidering them, which I find fascinating. Could it be that these traditional therapeutic treatments may in fact have a place in contemporary healthcare? And if so, what does that tell us about the nature of scientific investigation?

I'd like to share the type of work being done in my own faculty. Currently, my colleagues and I are investigating ancient remedies using natural ingredients. In order to do this, we've been analysing ancient medical books containing notes and recipes for various treatments. Now, obviously we're primarily interested in the medical applications of the notes, but unless we understand the historical context, it's virtually impossible to make sense of the treatments.

For this reason, we're now collaborating with experts in the history and literature faculties to understand the notes and source materials better. In the first instance, we asked for their linguistic support so that we could translate the materials. However, we subsequently realised that our colleagues could provide useful socio-economic insights too. For instance, they helped us understand the religious significance of some of the remedies. They also explained how the trade of key ingredients used to operate globally.

Many of the treatments we've discovered so far are for conditions that thankfully no longer affect people, either because of improvements in diet and sanitation or due to medical advances. As expected, the treatments we've translated were found to prescribe the use of herbs, spices, animal organs and even some metals. Some of the treatments involved substances that doctors would never prescribe now because they are known to be poisonous, regardless of whether they were ever effective.

However, it's worth underlining that ancient remedies should not be dismissed entirely. We found examples of treatments that still exist today, albeit in different forms. And what's particularly interesting is that some of the treatments involve techniques or ingredients that doctors stopped using centuries ago, yet which are now on the verge of being brought back.

The substantial use of animal organs in ancient medicine may seem unpleasant to many modern societies, but actually, there's a growing debate amongst doctors today about the possibility of using animal organs in certain forms of surgery. And the ancient use of copper for eye conditions is something that scientists are now looking to update because this metal does indeed have therapeutic properties.

If we can draw inspiration from ancient medicine, and improve them using our advanced knowledge, then surely, there's the chance to have the best of both worlds.

Part 3

Audio track: C1_Listening_6_3.mp3

Part 3. You hear an interview in which two theatre performers, Karl Myers and Lucy Westbrook, are talking about their work. For questions 15 to 20, choose the best answer: A, B, C or D.

Interviewer	Hello everyone. Joining me today are Karl Myers and Lucy Westbrook currently starring in the play *The Sword*. It's quite a departure from your trademark comedy work, isn't it?
Speaker 1	Well, my reputation for serious drama has been developing, but yes, I've never appeared in such a major production before. It's certainly the hardest thing I've ever done professionally, and I'm enjoying it immensely. The response from audiences has been brilliant, hasn't it, Karl?
Speaker 2	Definitely! It's such a well-known play with no special twists or shocks in it, so fans of my comedy were surprised when I joined the cast. But like Lucy, it's really pushed me to my performance limits. It's great to see critics and theatre-goers responding favourably.
Interviewer	And it's another play where we hear Lucy's wonderful singing voice.
Speaker 1	Haha! Yes, my last play featured lots of songs, which I was very nervous about! Actually, had it not been directed by Ronald Spearman, I probably wouldn't have agreed to be in it! But I couldn't pass up the chance to work with someone I'd respected for such a long time, whatever the part. During rehearsals, his guidance and feedback really helped me figure out the character I was playing and move from just reading lines from a script to really connecting with the character.
Interviewer	It must be great to work in such a supportive environment.
Speaker 1	Absolutely. We all give each other professional advice. Not that I always follow it! I mean, there's still too much prejudice against TV work. It's so irritating that many of my peers regard it as inferior to performing on stage. But anyway, you have to be quite thick-skinned and follow your own path to make it in this industry. Many of us

have had years of people telling us to find a more secure career instead, especially in smaller towns where performing isn't necessarily viewed as a legitimate career.

Interviewer   Karl, what's your take?

Speaker 2   Well, Lucy's point about prejudice is interesting because we aren't trained like that in our degrees. We're exposed to a wide range of performance styles and modes. That's actually vital, because not every graduate will have the chance to work with their chosen directors or producers. But it's a pity that drama degrees don't provide more training on the daily reality of the industry too – you know, like financial matters. If they did, that might give more students the confidence to apply, especially those that have no family connection to the performing arts.

Interviewer   So, being a performer isn't all glamour and excitement, then?

Speaker 1   Hardly! It's a bit like being a sports star. A lot of people envy them but forget about all the sacrifices they make to get to the top.

Speaker 2   That's a really interesting comparison, Lucy. And I'd go further and say it's not just the top athletes or famous performers. Most people have no real idea about what it's like to work in professional sport or the arts at any level. Not that I need anyone's sympathy, of course. I'm extremely fortunate to be making a living from doing something I love.

Interviewer   Well, your passion's clear to see in all your work, Karl. But what's it like to play such an unpleasant character in *The Sword*?

Speaker 2   Well, credit goes to the wardrobe department for helping me transform into such a scary-looking villain! But seriously, there's a lot to be said for taking risks and being willing to play characters that the audience won't necessarily like, I see it as my main strength, actually. My approach is to identify something I appreciate or admire about the character. That way, I can add extra dimensions people won't expect.

Part 4

Audio track: C1_Listening_6_4.mp3

Part 4. You hear five short extracts in which people are talking about learning to drive. For questions 21 to 30, choose from the list A–H.

Extract 1

I didn't rush to get my driving licence and my own car because, in my town, everything's on my doorstep or a short bus ride away. But I eventually got fed up of limiting my travel plans because I was reliant on public transport. Getting a car would open up so many more options. But of course, when you've spent years using public transport, you don't give things like insurance, tax, car maintenance and fuel costs a second thought. I hadn't appreciated how much of a financial burden car ownership can be! That's why I don't use my car as much as I'd expected.

Extract 2

Living in a commuter town is pretty convenient because there are decent rail links to the capital. But I want the chance to get involved in a greater variety of engineering projects in different parts of the country. That's why getting a driving licence was a must for me. It's certainly been the right decision for me professionally, but I wouldn't say I enjoy driving. In fact, most days I hate it. There are so many inconsiderate drivers on the road. I wonder if they act so selfishly when they're not driving? I'm surprised some of them have even passed their test.

Extract 3

I've only learnt to drive recently and I didn't enjoy the process at all. I found it hard to learn all the theory, and I only passed the test on my third attempt. I'm not a confident driver. I don't enjoy going long distances in the car, but fortunately I rarely need to do that because my office is near enough that I can still commute by train. Really, I learnt to drive to help out my parents. They're getting older and it's easier for me to run errands for them if I can drive. I know they really appreciate it.

Extract 4

People are surprised I only learnt to drive in my fifties. It's always been something I've dreamt of doing. When I was a kid, I imagined having all sorts of adventures in cars! Sadly though, I couldn't afford driving lessons, and then I moved from country to country, so I didn't have time to learn. But on my fiftieth birthday, I decided it was finally time to get my licence and get a cheap car. I love not having to ask friends and family for lifts now. You might think that's a minor thing, but it's a source of great pride for me.

Extract 5

I know the motor industry has to do more about air pollution, and obviously, walking and cycling are greener, healthier alternatives for short journeys. But I'm not going to apologise for being what my friends call a 'petrol-head'. Cars aren't things that are used just to get from place to place, they're fantastic feats of engineering! I originally got my licence mainly because I was curious about mechanics and how cars worked. And now, there's nothing better than going for a long scenic drive, listening to my favourite music. For me, it's the same feeling that a sports fan gets when their team wins.

How to download the audio

To download the accompanying audio files, please visit our website:

prosperityeducation.net/c1-listening-audio-download

Use the password TIAB to access this page.

Click on the book image to download the audio.

The audio file size for all six tests is approximately 180MB.

Leave us a review

By the way, if you enjoy our book, it would be great if you could leave us a review on Amazon. We're a small publisher and every review makes a difference to us and to our lovely team of authors :-)

Made in United States
Troutdale, OR
03/06/2024